Me, Myself And
My Arranged Marriage

By: Natasha Asghar

Me, Myself and My Arranged Marriage

ISBN : 978-1-5272-0600-7

Front cover designed by: Oliver Lavery-Farag

Printed by Elite Publishing Academy

TABLE OF CONTENTS

FORWARD

I would like to dedicate this to my parents for their constant patience with me, my nearest and dearest friends for listening to these endless tales over and over again and for all the single men and women out there who genuinely believe in love. But have been so badly hurt in their relationship(s) that they're questioning their own sanity. I can assure you there is NOTHING wrong with you!!

We live in a world where there are a lot of lovely people: some good, some bad and some very strange. Just keep your chin up. The right one for you will make an appearance soon enough.

Special thank you to Jay Patel, Jigna, Shai and Ollie for all of your help and support with the editing and designs.

My name is Nikki, I am twenty-six years old and live in London. I am an only child and have a lovely set of parents. By profession my dad is an Accountant/Politician and my mum is a Doctor. They have been in the UK for forty years and are fairly moderate when it comes to religion. My parents had what some would call a fairy tale romance. Every year the High Commission in London hold an independence Day ceremony and many moons ago my dad went as a guest, my mum was a delegate with my grandfather and I've been told by my dad's friends that when he saw my mum waltz in with her sari on he simply could not take his eyes off of her. He even pointed at her and told them "There is the woman I will marry." Lo and behold! Thirty something years later after a number of trials and tribulations they are happily married.

As an only child everyone always used to ask me, "so I guess you must be really really spoilt then?" But truthfully I was blessed with two amazing parents who doted on me, I never had four or five holidays a year or anything I asked for. I had two parents who loved me and trusted me not to do anything stupid and tried their best to teach me the value of money- Although this went out the window every time there was a sale in Harrods.

From a very young age, I swore that I would not have sex before marriage and to this day I have stood by my word as I personally want to save something for the man I marry. However my story of finding a husband has been an epic ordeal that will certainly have you in stitches.

As an Asian girl it is quite common for a young girl to receive proposals from a young age, and mine started when I was eighteen and at a family wedding. One of the Aunties said to my mum "I really like Nikki and would like to take her home for my son" as though I was a piece of furniture at IKEA! My parents both believe that a girl should be educated enough to be able to stand on her own two feet. So my mum kindly informed the Aunty that I was too young and still had to complete University. After I completed

University, my parents and my lecturer (who surprise surprise was from the sub Indian continent too) ganged up on me and gave me an ultimatum on my graduation day. Whilst most of my friends were out getting drunk and disorderly after the ceremony I was being given severe words...

"Either get married...or do a Masters."

So like any 'normal' twenty one year old I chose to do the Masters on the condition that I would be able to live my life, follow my career and dreams until the age of twenty-five. This was because I felt that twenty-five was a relatively decent age to settle down, and think about 'settling down and being more family orientated.'

Let me bring you in on a little secret EVERY Asian parent wants their children to get married and have children. That is their ultimate goal, because when they die and they go and face Allah, Bhagvan, Buddha, Guru ji or even Jesus they want to be able to say "I did my duty as a parent and got my children married off and settled". So in reality even if

Asian parents make a promise -believe me - they are ALL telling porkies! This is because as soon as they see a nice Asian boy or are told about one, they get a serious case of self-inflicted amnesia and all promises about living life for a while go out of the window.

Over the last few years I have been introduced to hundreds of men from various backgrounds, personalities, professions and parts of the world. Being an Asian I know culturally some of my non-Asian friends find the whole arranged marriage process fascinating, others cannot believe what torturous activities our families put us through. It really upsets me when I see on television 'arranged marriages' are always seen as young Asian women being forced to marry men who they don't know or even have anything in common with. Their parents drag them off to the sub-Asian continent, steal their passports and force them to marry off their daughters, nieces and cousins.

I have the utmost sympathy for these men and women. As I have always been in an incredibly fortunate position. In my culture it is very common for us to marry our cousins. I know that sounds really gross, it's not a concept I am keen on, however I know a lot of people are still keen on the idea of keeping relations strong within the family. When I was born my Chachee (Dad's brother's wife) came to visit me at the Hospital and said to my mum "I hope you keep Nikki tucked away for me, as I want her for my son when she's older." My dad was out-raged by such a statement and announced "NO, I swear that whichever man Nikki lays her hand on and says 'Dad I want to marry him' that is and shall be the ONLY man she marries." True to his word he has never ever forced me to marry someone. I always get quite upset when I hear about parents forcing their children to be in relationships that they never wanted or are forced to form relations with people they do not love or even when they are in love with someone else. So I am going to portray how the process behind a REAL arranged marriage in the UK takes place.

I have been introduced to so many men that if I dedicated a chapter to each and every one then I would need to sign a deal for my own version of the Encyclopaedia Britannica. But I am going to dedicate a chapter to eight of the men I have met and how they have all taught me something about myself and more about the whole arranged/love marriage process and I hope my experiences will prepare you for the journey you will embark upon or the one you have taken already. (For the purpose of this book their (real) names and identities have been changed.)

THE UNI BOY

I met Aron when I was studying for my Masters, even though my parents had promised they would not pester me about marriage in true desi (Asian) style they had "a guy that was amazing and I HAD to meet." Now it's quite normal that when a guy comes round to check a girl out for a 'rishta' (proposal) purpose the girl's family have to bend over backwards in the hospitality stakes and in true form my parents have never failed to amaze me.

Aron lived in North London, I was twenty two and he was twenty six, he was six foot tall and attractive, had a nose that would put a pelican to shame and when he came to the house he wore a black suit, pink shirt and no tie, so clearly the boy meant business. He worked as an Accountant for a lucrative company in the city. When he came round he bought his mum, dad and two sisters. They all seemed very nice and polite, they bought flowers and chocolates, which is always a good sign as I come from the belief that you should never go to someone's house empty handed for the first time.

My mother had prepared a feast, when they arrived I was made to adorn a shalwar kameez (a traditional Indian/Pakistani dress) which my mum had just bought back from Pakistan. After meeting the family I was asked to bring in the tea, coffee, samosas, spring rolls, biscuits, cake and any other paraphernalia my mother and I had conjured up in the kitchen.

After chatting about the weather, our family backgrounds and politics, we then sat down for dinner, where my mum had literally not spared anything. We had about six dishes laid out which included pilau, chicken curry, lamb saag, potato curry, daal, channe (chickpeas) and naan bread for anyone who does not like pilau.

After dinner my mum was asked if I could spend some *quality time* thus one on one time with Aron in the dining room, which was centrally placed in the house. Whilst we were having some 'private time' both sets of parents and his sisters went in the front room. We sat and chatted about University, his family, his views on the future, and he was determined to live with his family, as he had lived out of home for a short period of time and could not cope without his Mum's cooking! All the while knowing that everyone was listening to the conversation, it was awkward but being such a loud mouth it was fine with me. The conversation became a tad more serious when we spoke about future living arrangements. Personally I do not have any issue living with in-laws and as the conversation developed I could tell that we were getting on famously, however I just sat there thinking '*Oh my God I am too young to settle down! How could I possibly get married at the age of 22!*' Before we got up to join the rest of the family he actually said the nicest thing to me, which to this day no one had ever said '*Nikki, you're a wonderful girl and whatever happens between us, make sure you never settle.*'

I must be honest, he was extremely genuine however his lack of ambition was a real turn off. I was

14

a fresh graduate, was oozing with ambition and I have always sought someone who is equally if not more ambitious and entertaining than me. However I sadly did not see this in Aron, he was quite happy to 'stay in the same job until he retired, as that is what Dad did.' Which left me stunned? He was very respectful to my mother and held doors open for her, after my mother stuffed his entire family to the brim with her samosas and spring rolls, they left.

Now normally if a guy is interested his family contact the girl's family and say they had a lovely time and would like to invite her and her family round for the same treatment at their house.

This did happen and as though on cue, Aron's father called our house within twenty four hours of leaving and thanked my parents for their hospitality and invited us all round for dinner, at a later date. Now, I have a major issue, as I do not like to lead people on. Since I have no brothers and sisters, I am a trial and error guinea pig for my parents in that Aron was my first 'rishta' proposal. They followed correct etiquette and promised to visit the following week. However, I felt terrible. There was simply no spark between Aron and myself, so the following week I conveniently developed a stomach bug, and consequently could not go. So my parents went to their house and when they returned, they made me feel even worse by telling me that Aron had made such an effort to look good and was genuinely so disappointed by the fact that I was not there. I felt horrible, not only for the stomach bug but also for the fact that I should feel guilty. So I explained to my parents that I didn't wish to progress any further with Aron, as I couldn't feel we were compatible on any level. So the following day, my father called them to say thank you for a lovely evening. He said *'You are a lovely family, however on this occasion I feel Nikki and Aron are not compatible'* and that was the end of that.

THE GOLD DIGGER

Shahid was my second official proposal and actually came as a recommendation from my Uncle. My mum is the eldest of her siblings and they all have the utmost respect for her. We had gone to my Uncle's house for a long weekend and for some strange reason, my cousin and my Uncle took me to Finchley Park for 'a walk.' Being young and naïve I genuinely thought we were going to the park for a walk. Little did I know that my Uncle and cousin had other plans. Turns out that my Uncle knew about a woman who had two sons - the eldest had got married to a girl from the homeland and the youngest was a lecturer at a University. They came from Manchester and as he was thirty they wanted to marry him off as soon as possible. They had sent a very, very close up picture of Shahid and were insisting on coming to the house. Now I must admit that I did not find Shahid very attractive - he was geeky looking (no offence to geeks) but he had rodent-like looks and wore big thick glasses. And even if I put the looks aside, for some reason my sixth sense was not in tune with this proposal.

Now you are probably thinking that this girl does not sound in tune with the whole marriage concept at all. But I'm actually quite the opposite. I used to be a true romantic and believed in finding 'the one.' But after meeting numerous players, liars, cheaters and bigots. I began to believe the old fashioned way was probably the best way.

After having cried my eyes out and being convinced by my dad (the one person who I never say no to), I agreed to have Shahid and his family around for dinner.

When he arrived he was six foot tall, quite skinny, he had that whole hair slicked to the left look going on and seemed like a real nerd. He didn't say much apart from 'hi/hello'. I came down in the whole Indian outfit, did the whole tea making routine. However, since my Uncle had initiated this whole thing, he and my younger cousin Tara came for moral support. More so for my mother than me, as she takes this whole affair so seriously and when potential suitors visit the house she tends to get quite stressed out about food, dessert etc. "Presentation is key" as she loves to say.

Shahid came dressed in a pink shirt and black suit, and bought his married brother along for moral support, whose wife was due to come from the Motherland any day once her visa was sorted. His mother was quite aged and came dressed in a traditional Asian suit and seemed quite backwards in her tone and etiquette. Once again I had to serve the tea, coffee, samosas and biscuits with a smile. In all honesty, I was not in the mood for this pow-wow but nonetheless I put on a brave face and sat with them. They asked 'What do you do? Where do you live?' The usual formalities. I forced a smile and ushered them to the table. My Cousin was only fourteen and she was getting annoyed as Shahid's elder brother kept calling her 'Tara baji' (baji is a term we use for elder sister). It was so ridiculous yet hilarious at the same time, as he was double her age.

We had dinner, and I have to say, I know I'm not a Miss World of any sort but Shahid had the worst teeth I had ever seen in my life and after a couple of hours I knew this was a lost cause. However, I give my mother full points as she did everything she could to try and make it work.

After the meal was over, my parents, Shahid and his family moved into the front room. I was in the kitchen putting dishes in the dishwasher and my mother came in and said "Shahid wants to talk to you." I ran into the utility room and started shaking my head as she tried to send me off to talk like a lamb to the slaughter. We then moved into the dining room, which is linked to my parents Kitchen and sat opposite each other. The he proceeded to ask "so what do you want in a life partner, Nikki?" I clearly knew this would not be going anywhere so replied "I want a tall, handsome man who is from a wonderful family and will keep me happy."

He then smiled with his crooked teeth and said "me too". Then he asked me when I was looking to get married? My response was "not for the next few years at least." Which is not really the done thing and also a standard brush off. Most people don't beat around the bush when they are really interested in someone. However I just wanted him to leave. Then he asked 'do you have any brothers or sisters?' Which I don't, so I responded by saying 'I am an only child.' He then said something to me that I will never forgive or forget. He started looking around my parents dining room and turned towards me and said "So Nikki, I assume that one day all of this, you know, the house, the cars etc.. Will be yours?" Now I may not have a PHD like Shahid, but I was disgusted. My father always said to be the best host when people are round, but I swear I wanted to slap this man six ways to Sunday. I could not believe that I had been sitting in front of such a blatant gold digger. I always heard they existed but I never knew someone could ever be so cold and heartless.

After that comment I jumped out of my chair and said "we should go into the Living room." We walked in to an unexpected pin drop silence. After they left I was so angry that my dad had to take me for a drive. He asked "what did you think of the dude?" I've been quite cold about first meetings but learnt and seen that it's never a good idea to ever be keen about someone you don't even know. So my dad and I refer to every potential suitor as "dude".

I was livid and started screaming. "What a freaking waste of time and space! You guys made me waste my weekend for that loser who only wanted to get his grubby paws on your house and cars". My dad was dumbstruck. He looked at me with shock and dismay but consoled me that's it's never going to happen.

Then I said 'Daddy how come there was a tense atmosphere when I came back into the living room?" To which he replied "I have never met such a low and disgusting family." When I asked him to elaborate, he said "Shahid had been married before and they did not want to tell us in case we said no to the meeting." Dad was disgusted and gave my mother and uncle a piece of his mind. Now my father does not discriminate against divorcees however he and I both despise liars and deceitful people.

I found it very hard to hide my look of disgust the following day when Shahid's mother called to thank my parents for their hospitality and actually had the gaul to say they wanted to "take the matter further." My father was livid. He felt betrayed, annoyed, dismayed and angry that people like this actually exist. From that day forward, I learnt that there are people in the world who are wolves dressed in sheep's clothing. I realised that there are also people who are snakes dressed in sheep's clothing too.

THE WANNABE SOCIALITE

At this point in my life I was getting rather disenchanted by the whole 'arranged' marriage process, so my parents hired a new introducer who had a theory. When a girl is young, the proposals will flood in. However when she becomes an old maid, no one will want her. I know it sounds rather narrow minded, however even in the twenty-first century, many people still have these outdated views.

The new introducer, was a man who sent the details of potential suitors to my mum's mobile with the name of the parents and their phone number. It was then up to my parents, or the suitor's parents to contact one another and to find out more.

When my mother called Irfan's parents, she was informed that he was a Barrister in the city of London, drove a Ferrari and had a house in the country. But he was a year younger than me. Now I personally do not like younger men. It is nothing

24

personal, and I do not have any disrespect for women who like a younger man but I would have preferred someone older.

I saw Irfan's picture and heard his credentials - he was born and raised in London, educated in Harvard, graduated the top of his class and came back to the UK to be signed up to a top legal firm in the city. On paper this boy clearly ticked the boxes. From his pictures, he seemed nice, well-dressed, tall, dark and seemed like a laugh.

As usual, my parents invited him and his parents to our house for dinner. I had to adorn a nice, white, traditional shalwar kameez and I must say on immediate appearance I was not very impressed as he had really bad teeth - not that I have a tooth fetish or anything, I just feel it is important to not have fangs hanging outside your mouth.

Irfan came in a nice dark grey suit and pink shirt, with black shoes. I must say he dressed very well. Turned out he was an only child, enjoyed travelling, especially to Pakistan (which I found bizarre) and to my horror he did not even flinch when I mentioned my love for extreme sports. Co-incidentally they came three days before my birthday and Irfan and I chatted for ages. He seemed sincerely interested in my family, our lives etc etc. I was planning on spending my birthday in Wales. I am a huge birthday celebrator and like mine to go on for as long as humanly possible. So I normally start my celebrations with a family dinner and then continue with friends, colleagues and acquaintances. When he was made aware as to the seriousness of my birthday and its importance to me, he started asking what I had planned this year. So I told him that I had asked for an 'EXTREME' birthday. So Day one: horse riding, Day 2: clay pigeon shooting, Day 3: target shooting and Day: 4 collapse and get ready for a hectic weekend with friends.

I must say Irfan was quite forward. He asked me for my phone number as soon as our parents were out of earshot, and promised to keep in touch. I must admit that the day they came I had been recovering from the flu from hell - honestly nose-streaming, greasy hair, body aches - I truly looked more like death walking as opposed to a hot, young, sexy rishta-girl. I could feel my flu getting worse throughout the morning, but just had to hang in there, as under no circumstances should a girl appear to look or be ill, even if it's a cold as it may appear that she's not always healthy.

We sat together, covered the usual formalities, had food and when he asked what I had made, which was in fact chicken tikka, he took three helpings with a wink and seemed to enjoy it. They left after a few hours and we didn't hear from them, my poor mother was beginning to think I was telling these boys some stories such as being a secret alien, to prevent them being interested in me. But truthfully to this day I have never been nasty or disrespectful to anyone. As I was feeling so unwell, I honestly couldn't care less, so it didn't make an inch of a difference to me or my life.

On the day of my birthday I came home from an enchanting horse-riding session to find that he had in fact sent twenty-four long stemmed roses through a well-known florist to my parent's house. I thought it was my dad, as he seemed to have forgotten the auspicious day and had not said a word as he left for work in the morning. So when I saw the card with a really lovely note, I must say I was touched. My poor mother nearly passed out from shock. We stayed in touch over the next couple of weeks. He called me every day to find out how I was, what I was doing and every time we both chatted for ages. Irfan was positively fascinated with my father's side of the family.

You see my mother's family are all in the medical or teaching profession in Pakistan and my father's side are all Air Force men. Ranging from Air Vice Marshall's and Air Commodores, plus as I mentioned before, Irfan was infatuated with Pakistan. He loved the Punjab Club (which is the Ivy equivalent in Pakistan and membership is only available to elite members of the forces such as my uncle's) and he was fascinated by all of the places where my uncles and cousins spent their spare time, which really wasn't anything special to me. But to him, I may as well have said that I had life-long membership to The Ivy. He was entranced by this, and constantly asked how I felt coming from such a prestigious family? At this point 'gold digger' alarm bells were going off in my head, or maybe Irfan was just being a little over enthusiastic.

We promised to meet up when I got back to London, but when I returned some of my friends had arranged a surprise party for me. I had no idea where it would be? Who would be there? Or even when it started? Just that it would be in the evening and one of my friends was coming to my house to pick me up.

I believe in openness so when Irfan called I told him a party had been organised. He wished me the best and hoped I had a good time. A couple of hours later he started to text me: 'What are you up to? Glamming up I suppose?' To which my response was

'I've just ironed my clothes, my hair looks like an explosion has gone off and make up still to go.' He then called me, told me he was going out for fish and chips by himself. Now part of me felt really bad, but my friends had organised this party and I really had no idea where it would be, and in these sort of circumstances, the potential husband must not see you have a good time with your friends as you will get branded a 'party girl' who is not capable of managing a house and rearing sensible children.

So in case any such circumstances arose, I did not invite him, a decision I am very proud of now, as what followed will take your breath away...

Irfan began the conversation by asking in a very non-kinky and direct manner, what I would be wearing. I explained that 'I had a beautiful Julian Macdonald dress and some silver shoes and jewellery to match.' He then asked me how many children I wanted, which I must admit was a bit forward. I responded, by saying that 'I did not mind, and would love them regardless.' Irfan then said would you love them if 'our child went off with a white boy/girl?' My response was 'yes of course' I have no issues, as long as my children were happy. I come from a very large family and we often joke about being called the United Nations of families as we have numerous religions married in and out of the family, and I was and have always been proud of them.

Irfan then flipped out, he started telling me how important family was, to which I agreed, as my parents are my world. Irfan then turned around and said 'you know Nikki, your Mum's family clearly sounds very Chelsea and your Father's family are the Knightsbridge of the world.' I demanded a definition to which he replied 'I bet no one from your Father's side has settled for anyone below their breeding?' I got so angry at this point, I could have punched a wall. But I was cordial and said that my friend had arrived.

I then joined the rest of my friends for an amazing birthday celebration that I discovered my parents had secretly organised in central London for me. His behaviour had put me in a foul mood for the first hour, but then I decided to let my hair down and genuinely enjoyed my night.

The next day as on cue, Irfan called asking 'So what happened? Where did you all go?' To which I responded my parents organised a private function for me at Fifty. Now Fifty is an exclusive members club next to the Ritz in central London and somehow, my dad had seen how poorly I was prior to my birthday and consequently arranged the whole night for me. Now any 'normal' guy would say 'Wow, that's amazing.' But as he was still seething blood from not being invited, Irfan retorted by saying 'you're a proper bang-bang girl, aren't you Nikki!' At this point I went absolutely crazy.

I could not believe that a pathetic, self-centred, class-conscious, arrogant moron had the audacity to call me such a thing.

He then asked me to meet him for a dinner date that I had agreed to whilst I was in Wales and by this point was beginning to think it may have been due to the overdose of Night Nurse I had taken when delirious from the flu. So he decided that it would be nice to go to a restaurant close to his flat in Edgware Road. In conversation, he told me that he liked a woman that wore pearls. So in true Asian Jackie O style, I wore a pair of dark jeans, a black wraparound jumper, some Chanel pearls, a pair of cute silver ballet pumps and a pashmina for effect. It was mid-October at this point and quite warm. I arrived early as I have always had a major OCD problem with time, and can never be late for anything. As I arrived at Edgware Road I was twenty minutes early for the meeting and must admit it was probably the hardest meeting ever as I was still seething over the whole "bang-bang" comment. So I called my best friend Clair and literally had to make her give me three reasons why I should stay or go through a dinner I had no desire whatsoever to attend. Clair and I went to University together and she knows that I am going through the whole arranged marriage process. She is always asking me when the big day is so she knows when she can buy a hat. But she has always given me invaluable advice and even though she was busy, I called her in a panic and had to ask 'Can you give me three reasons why I should not turn around and go home? I had filled her in on the whole Knightsbridge/Chelsea/party girl/bang-bang comment. She was just as disgusted by his comment but reminded me that if I left, my parents respect would be undermined, which is something I could not bear.

As soon as I got off the phone, I texted Irfan to say 'I am here.' He replied 'I'll be there in 5' and true to his word he showed up after five minutes wearing dark jeans, a dark jumper, long black cashmere coat. We walked for about five minutes to a restaurant that he apparently 'loved.' So we arrived at the restaurant it was a quaint little Italian place and the waiters were very friendly. When we sat down at a very posh French restaurant, I sat on a long sofa towards the wall and Irfan sat on a chair opposite me. I ordered fish and he ordered chicken, we made pleasant conversation and he wanted to know about all the details from Saturday, which had not changed. But as a Barrister I guess he liked the idea of cross examining his potential wife to be, as well as clients.

Then he announced how he 'loved to sing.' And then out of the blue, started singing at me in the middle of this restaurant. I was positively mortified! At first I just smiled pleasantly, but then started to cringe. We chatted for ages and as he wore a long coat he laid it down next to me, on the sofa side, rather than let it get dirty on the chair. After a couple of hours, the waiter bought over a couple who were waiting to sit next to us. Now Irfan could not see them, but I could see that the coat was in their way. So I innocently picked it up to move it to my right side. At this exact moment, Irfan yelped 'What on earth do you think you're doing' as though I was about to steal it and run away. I was a tad gobsmacked at this point but rather calmly pointed to the waiter and couple standing behind him who were just as stunned by his response. The couple sat down next to us and we carried on chatting about work and his future aspirations, with a few Bollywood songs such as *Kabhi kabhi, meri sapno ki rani* and *rang barse* - which if you know Bollywood, you'll recall are all VERY VERY old songs.

Whilst singing a song older than the two of us, I noticed that he was checking out the girl on the table next to us. Now I'm not one of those insecure girls, who cannot handle a guy even looking at another girl. I am aware that men are not angels and like to 'check out' female talent. But I swear I have never been in the presence of a potential suitor practically drooling over a girl who isn't me. I was not infuriated by him looking at this red-haired Beth Ditto lookalike sitting across from us, but more at myself for having attended such a pathetic dinner, when my sixth sense clearly knew it was going to be a bad idea.

I then looked at my watch and saw it was 11pm, which was quite late.

He asked me how I planned to get home, to which I responded 'the tube'. He said 'Okay.' That was it. He never once offered to take me home, or even call a cab. I like a man to be a man and take care of women when they are in such company, and sadly Irfan did not live up to this claim which he appeared to pride himself in.

I asked if he could walk me to the tube station as it was nearly midnight and we were quite a distance from the main road and as I had no desire to be mugged or worse on a Thursday evening. So on the way to the station he sang a few more Bollywood songs, which in all honesty were really starting to get on my nerves.

As soon as we got to the station we said our goodbyes and I swore that moment that I would never contact Irfan again. I got home at midnight and called my parents and told them about his lame public audition for X-Factor and all of the comments that had been passed.

I know there are people who are intelligent, well-mannered and rich, but there are a lot of people out there who are very status conscious.

It is not something that my family and I consider to be a valuable trait but there are a lot of people who wish to marry into families which will raise their profile and give them status in society by allowing them to gloat at gatherings, who their in-laws are. The whole experience showed me that there are a lot of class-conscious people out there, but when that is all they see, let them go as they aren't interested in the real you. All they want is a hand up into social circles. More importantly, if a man insults you and above all your family, he's not worth it.

THE IRISH ONE

Now I must admit I am incredibly sceptical when it comes to online dating and introducers. My parents are well aware of this fact. A couple of years ago, my mother asked me to take a weekend off from work. As I worked in the banking sector, we were forced to work every other Saturday. I must admit it did not go down well with my boss, but he agreed. My mum told me 'We are going to meet some of your dad's friends.' Which sounded a little bit strange as I know all of my father's friends.

Saturday came along and I walked downstairs in a pair of skinny jeans, a nice shirt and green bomber jacket. My mother took one look at me and said 'right go back upstairs and get changed.' Now normally that sort of outfit would be fine to meet with Dad's friends, but on this occasion she shouted at me to put some 'decent clothes on.' I went to my bedroom and cried.

My dad, heard me sobbing and came in to my bedroom and calmly explained that we were actually going to meet a bachelor - they did not know his name or anything else. But the lady in the marriage bureau said he would be 'a perfect match.' Dad then asked if I would 'kindly get dressed as we had to go as soon as possible, this was because he was specially flying in from Dublin to see me. But he reassured me as he always had done, that if for any reason I am not happy with this or any other match then he will support me one hundred per cent of the way and not let anything happen without my consent.

I was so upset with my mum for not telling me the plan and then sending me to get changed, so I decided to dress for the occasion. I put on a pair of shorts, leg-warmers and black trousers and I wore a black woollen vest, a gold vest top, another back top, with a golden cardigan and a 'LARGE' black and white three quarter length coat. As it was November, I knew my mother would never ask me to show her what

I was wearing underneath, so I thought if I dressed like the female equivalent to the Michelin Tyre monster, the 'dude' would run away.

We arrived to a dingy old house in East London, which is the hub of this particular establishment. It was cold and my parents walked in first. His mother was there and the marriage bureau lady sat us all down and sat behind us on an old oak desk. She read out our credentials, names, hobbies, parent's names and then said 'Let us all give the children some space, so we'll send them into another room and allow them to get to know each other.'

Without any shadow of a doubt, Harris is probably the only one guy that truly made a lasting impression on me. He was six foot tall, good-looking, handsome, dressed well in a pair of jeans, a white shirt and a maroon blazer. He did take my breath away. We sat and chatted for ages and inside I was kicking myself for looking like a total plonker!

Harris was a businessman. His family owned their own textile factory in Dublin. He was incredibly ambitious, educated, liked travelling, appeared to know about worldly affairs and above all else had a VERY sexy Irish accent. We talked about our social lives and admittedly he liked to party and go out with his friends, which is normally a taboo in these situations by the girl and boy. After an hour and a half of general chit-chat, the marriage bureau *Aunty* came in and told us our time was up. We walked out as though we were being led to the Headmistress's office for some form of punishment. But our parents said their farewells and we just nodded as hugging, kissing on the cheek and shaking hands can be deemed inappropriate in these situations.

On the way home, my parents wanted some sort of feedback and I said I thought he was lovely and would like to know him a bit more. But I am quite superstitious in these sorts of matters, so I wanted to wait until we heard feedback from the family. A couple of days went by and my parents had not heard anything so they e-mailed the marriage bureau. The bureau Aunty basically said, the family loved my parents, they thought I was funny, bubbly and intelligent, but '*however Nikki is a bit too fat for Harris*.' I must say, I nearly died of shame. I was upset for days, and utterly inconsolable. I told my colleagues and friends about what had happened as they were intrigued to know how my weekend went. When I told them, they were stunned at the reason why.

The moral of my experience with Harris is that you never know when you may unexpectedly meet someone you actually like. So always look hot, make an effort because you just never know when you'll meet your mister right.

Above all, try not to dress like a Michelin 'tyre' woman as being called too fat by your potential mother in law is not a nice way to receive rejection and still haunts me to this day.

THE APPRENTICE ADDICT

Kaz and I were introduced by an introducer. Now these desi introducers charge money from people and then for X amount of pounds you get to meet a number of girls and boys.

However, this introducer did not believe in exchanging photos. He believed in getting the girl and boy to speak to each other directly. One evening, I received a phone call from my mum telling me to call a young man called Kaz.

Kaz was apparently a six-foot, fair accountant who lived in Windsor. His parents lived in Bristol and somehow knew my parents through family friends. Anyway, Kaz and I began talking. He told me that he loved to box, had lived abroad for a couple of years, really loved the Apprentice and enjoyed renovating properties in his spare time.

His mother had spoken to mine and when my mother requested a photograph, his mother told mine 'just tell Natasha to take one.' Quite clearly this woman thought that I had nothing better to do with my time than take some random guy's picture in a public place and send it to my mum. This initially really bothered my mum.

Kaz and I spoke on the phone every Thursday before 9pm, as he seemed to only be able to fit me in before his beloved programme *'The Apprentice'* was due to begin. He seemed really nice on the phone and had the strangest welsh accent I may have ever heard, which I will admit make me chuckle a little as I never heard an Asian guy with such a strong accent before.

Initially we spoke on the phone for a couple of weeks and arranged to meet up. He suggested we meet in Newport (the city where my parents live) for a coffee. The thought of this made me break out in a sweat as for me, Newport is a VERY small place. Everyone knows my parents and I really did not want to be spotted out with 'a boy' and then discussed by others. I like a certain level of privacy and so do my parents, so I suggested we meet in a restaurant at the

Celtic Manor. It's a hotel/restaurant close to my house and somewhere that would give us a chance to talk. He told me that his family had gone to the beach for the day, so we grabbed a couple of drinks and sat outside. I wore a pair of leggings and a nice red and black Chinese dress. I figured this guy was educated, so he would not be horrified by such an outfit. After sitting on the balcony for half an hour I thought I may catch hypothermia. After seeing my goose-bumps, Kaz suggested we sit inside, so we proceeded inside and then ordered cake. He ordered some strawberry number that turned out to be disgusting. I ordered a chocolate cake, which was incredibly tasty. We chatted about everything and talked about school, work, and family. He told me he had three sisters - only one was married, with kids and the other two were 'still looking.'

He was looking for someone modern and had no specific questions to ask me. Initially we agreed to meet for a couple of hours. Eventually I looked at the clock and six hours had passed. I genuinely had no idea where the time went. We said our goodbyes, he walked me to my car, and we said we would speak soon.

We stayed in touch, he was a tad useless at texting back, and often would take the whole day to reply, which I must admit is a BIG pet peeve of mine. But we agreed to meet up again and I thought why not? He didn't repulse me to the core and we had good banter.

For our second so-called 'date' we went out for dinner to a restaurant not very far from my place in London, but in an area very close to certain members of my family. Now we Asians have a certain rule - we do not normally discuss matters such as marriage until the ring is about to go on the finger and I must admit I am not really superstitious but I do believe in an Asian superstition called *'buri nazar'* - some may call it the evil eye - and I do believe it exists. When a person gloats, acts arrogantly, sings and dances about something from the roof-tops, then something normally goes wrong. So I was a little nervous, but we went out for dinner, I ordered a nice mixed grill and he ordered a chicken item from the menu as he wanted to keep his protein up for boxing! Apparently, he was some super champion, but I never had the opportunity to check him out in a pair of speedo styled shorts, pummelling a Hulk Hogan wannabe in a boxing ring. Again we had a decent conversation, it flowed and we seemed to be getting on well.

For the next meeting he suggested we meet up, but this time wanted to introduce me to his sister! When I told my mum she went loopy, as from her point of view she had not seen the boy, met the boy, or his family and I was being 'checked out' by the whole clan. Apparently, all of this was against Asian etiquette, as traditionally the boy's parents are supposed to come to our house, bond with my parents, chat about politics, the weather, the economy and current affairs. My mother would have prepared a five course meal with all the trimmings and genuinely been the hostess with the mostess. In this case, none of these things had taken place so resultedly my mother was livid.

We then went to an Italian restaurant where I met his sister Sana. She allowed us to have dinner in peace and then showed up around dessert time. We sat for coffee in the sweltering heat and made small talk about the weather and our childhood. It turned out she went to one of the Schools I attended when we lived in Cardiff. After we said our goodbyes, Kaz walked me to my car and we agreed to meet again.

A week later we planned to meet in central London. This was a tad awkward as I lived up north, but was told by my mother that I should be more open minded and go and meet him. I must admit at this point I was beginning to think this man was gay!

Based on the evidence that he took great pride in his appearance and confessed that his favourite album in the whole world was Girls Aloud's Greatest Hits, I put my niggling feeling aside and agreed to keep everyone happy. Kaz and I agreed to meet in Piccadilly at six o'clock, he showed up late (which is perhaps one of the worst things a man can do with me as I find when someone is late they are disrespecting the others time. I have no problems with emergencies and transport problems, but at least the other person should know.) When he finally showed up, Kaz insisted that we went on a 'little trip.' We got in a cab and to my surprise we ended up outside the London Eye. Now I have already been on the London Eye so for me it is just a big, more scenic Ferris Wheel. However, he was adamant that we went for a ride on the Eye. We got into a pod with a family of four, a newly married couple who were all over each other like a rash, and the two of us. And you will not believe what was going to happen next.

We were looking at all of the sights across London. I must admit it really was not romantic and seriously lacked any ambiance. As we reached the top of the eye, Kaz said 'Nikki can I ask you a question?' to which I replied *'Sure, anything, ask away?'* At this point, Kaz went down on one knee and pulled out a Tiffany's box. Before his knee hit the ground, I stopped him and whilst ushering him midway off the floor told him 'I really don't think this is the most appropriate place to do this.' Even if it is truthfully my dream to have a Tiffany's engagement ring. He looked pretty hurt, but he put the box away and went quiet.

After we completed our 360 degrees on the London Eye, we went to Chinatown for food, and sat outside in a really quaint Chinese restaurant. We made small talk for a while and I thanked him for a ride on the Eye. But eventually the inevitable happened and he pulled out the box again and opened it, I must say if I was a gold-digger I would have leapt up for joy as it was a six carat, Tiffany's square cut, platinum ring. I admit I did drool a bit, and the American tourists sitting next to us started screaming *'OH MY GOD HE'S GONNA PROPOSE TO THE GIRL, YOU GO HUNNI.'* Even though I had my own team of cheerleaders sitting and jeering for me on the next table to say 'yes' I closed the box and said 'Kaz I am really flattered you thought of me for marriage, but we've only met each other three times and you have not even met my parents! It's a bit too soon and I do not feel that I know you well enough.' He then turned around and said 'Yes Nikki, maybe you are right. I just thought it would be the most appropriate thing to do.'

We then ordered food, and as I was stuffed after my chicken Chow Mein, I did not have the room for dessert. However Kaz was craving a coffee and even though I did feel rather awkward in the circumstances I could not leave as that would be a sign of very bad manners.

Admittedly I was very surprised by Kaz's relaxed tone after I publically turned him down at the London Eye, and then later in Chinatown. But when the coffee arrived he said he wanted to say something to me. To which naturally I had no objection. Kaz then turned around and said 'I am really not happy with your lack of compassion toward me, you mentioned before when we first met that you liked 'to boogie' with your uncles and aunts at family weddings and parties.' Which in actual fact is true, I come from a very close family and whenever there is a function, we all have a great time. He said that he wanted his future wife not to dance around with her family, but make cups of tea for his dad. I was stunned and honestly it took all my strength not to lamp him in the face, but I hung in there. He then told me that he wanted to move back in with his parents and he felt that we would be a complete mismatch as he had planned within the last ten minutes that he would start to become a devout religious being and wanted a subservient, hijab-wearing, sister in Islam, which I clearly am not. He then asked me if he could drop me home. As you can imagine I naturally declined and said I'd rather get the tube home. I will admit that I got on the tube and cried my eyes out as I was so hurt by his narrow-minded and childish behaviour that it made me cry. I hate crying in public, but that day I let it all out. I then called my mum on the way home and told her what had happened. Her only response was 'Thank God he behaved in such an abhorrent manner.

I do not want him as a son-in-law anyway!' Which did make me feel better, but I really took a big blow, as I could not believe how something so innocent as having a good time with my family was being misconstrued by this narrow-minded boy.

So we closed the chapter on Kaz and never heard or saw him again. But it certainly has made me more cautious about men who want to move quicker than the wind, as there is usually always a hidden agenda and marriage is certainly something you cannot rush.

THE DENTIST WITH THE PAINFUL FATHER

The next bachelor's details were given to my parents by an introducer. I was told that he was a dentist living away from home, but his parents lived in London. When my mum was contacted by his father, she told me that he kept asking her "Does your daughter cook?' My mum thought it was a little strange but she answered yes - which is true. So even with our hectic work schedules it was difficult to arrange a day and time that was convenient for both families. I must admit I was a tad apprehensive as over the years I have learnt that 'some' mums and dads lie. When they say that their son "is six foot and well built" it usually means he is about five feet six, and a beanpole. When they say he likes to study, it usually means he wears four inch thick glasses, and when they say they want a "religious girl" it means their son is preparing to become a priest, so brace yourself.

I have learnt my lesson over the years and now ALWAYS make sure that my mum asks for a photo. Now I am not the type who judges men on their skin tone, as many Asians like their potential other half to be fair. I'm not bothered if a guy is darker, but I do not negotiate on height. I am five foot six and that is quite tall for an Asian girl, plus it would mean having to throw away about one hundred pairs of shoes. Which would be a massive sacrifice for me!

Before my mum invited this family round, she asked this particular contender's Dad for a photo, to which he said 'we do not believe in photos and we feel that we should meet each other. However my son does look a lot younger than he is.' Now at this point I had alarm bells going off in my head as the refusal of the photograph usually means the boy is not very attractive or, as my friends would say, 'it means he's butters.' To this day I have never laughed at a photo nor criticised anyone for not being photogenic, as not everyone looks like a model in photos. However the abrupt attitude by the boy's father was very off-putting. My parents live in Wales and always prefer potential suitors to come to their house. As I live in London, I would rather potential suitors and their families know where my real base is. This potential suitor's family were not willing to make their way to my parent's house in Wales, were quite abrupt in their manners and demanded to meet in London.

The second alarm bell went off when my mother asked 'What is your son's name?' She was told 'Madam I have not asked you your daughter's name so I don't feel it's appropriate for you to ask me your son's name. We will tell you when we meet. 'After a lot of arguments, especially as we did not have a name or face for the boy, we were told by the boy's father that his son would be home on a specific weekend and they would like to come to my house in London at four o'clock for tea. For the first time ever my mother had not put on the whole spread, which was an appreciated improvement. As the time was set for four, my parents and I woke up early. Dad left to see clients around London, and Mum and I went out to see some family and get my eyebrows done - a very important ritual in my life. Whilst exiting the salon at one o'clock with perfectly shaped eyebrows, my mum listened to her voicemail and looked like she had seen a ghost.

I asked her "what's the matter?" To my horror, she replied and said it was the boy's father saying that "they have to go to Birmingham in the afternoon and they would be showing up at our house at two o'clock." My poor mother started to panic as my dad was at least an hour away and none of us were showered, or even changed.

So we rushed home, Mum called Dad in a panic and told him to 'rush home.' She then called the boy's father and asked him, 'is everything okay?' To which he retorted 'We have to go up north and see other girls so we will be there as soon as possible.' My mother explained that we were all out of the house to which he responded 'That's okay, we can wait outside in the car for you.' At this point, my mother was beginning to lose her cool, as she likes these 'meetings' to be perfect. She explained that my father would like to be there for their arrival. At this point I assume 'the Uncle' got some shame, so everyone agreed that three o'clock would be a good time. So we all rushed home, had showers, I got dressed into one of my new traditional outfits and we waited for their arrival. At exactly three o'clock they arrived - Father, Mother and son. We were told that the young dentist's name was Adam, he's twenty-eight years old, and six foot tall. Now I openly admit to being five foot six and the fact that Adam came up to my cheek, clearly indicated that his father had told a seriously big porkie about his height and to top it off, he looked mal-nutritioned. We were told that he lives and works in a place not far from Birmingham. Which made me particularly angry as this place is not very far from my parents in Wales. What added more fuel to the fire was the comment by his parents that 'We visit him all the time.' So none of us could understand why they could not have made the trip to Wales. As soon as we sat down instead of Adam asking me anything, his father loudly and rather rudely asked 'So Nikki - can you cook? As our son misses home-cooked meals.' To which I answered 'Yes Uncle, I can cook.' Then Adam's Father asked me 'What do you do? What do you do in your spare time? Are you even willing to settle down?' I must admit I did feel as though I was being held as a prisoner of war and it infuriated my father when Adam's Father asked me twice after if I 'could cook.' I was beginning to get seriously irritated.

When he asked 'Nikki, what do you do in your spare time?' I replied 'Uncle I love to travel, go to the gym (which are really standard answers and then I brought out the big guns) and participate in extreme sports. So jumping out of a plane, jet skiing, Formula 1 racing and swimming with sharks give me a thrill. Now it is common etiquette amongst proposals not to declare that one likes to participate in such activities as the poor old aunties would have a heart failure as they expect to hear. 'In my spare time I like to perfect how to make the 'ideal round chapatti, not jet-ski around Jumeirah Beach with friends'

At this point, both of my parents started to stare at the floor they knew that I was not amused and was going to do anything in my power to put this family off.

His father also kept asking such probing questions such as 'Are you even ready to settle down?' to which I answered rather politely 'Uncle, believe me, if I was not ready to settle down I would not be here.' That clearly was not enough for him, as he continued to ask me 'Nikki, as you know the life of a locum is up and down, you seem to be a fairly career-orientated girl. Would you be happy to settle down and stay at home?'

Honestly this uncle was unlike any other uncle I had ever met before. He was such a dominant character, he made Stalin look like the tooth fairy. When I was offering them all tea, coffee and biscuits, Adam's mum would look at him. Until he said ' Take one', she would not take a biscuit from the plate. After three hours, which is a world record for most people when visiting for such purpose seem to stay for a minimum of eight to nine hours, they left and we all simultaneously breathed a sigh of relief.

I honestly do not know what to say about Adam and his family, as I was left incredibly peeved by the whole scenario. But it is worth bearing in mind, in an arranged marriage the saying 'a photo is worth a thousand words' has been created for a reason. Hence, rather than wasting time and energy it is always worthwhile to keep an open mind and **<u>ALWAYS get a picture!</u>**

THE ONE THAT GOT AWAY...THANK GOD!

Having gone through all of my previous experiences I like every woman out of luck with men began to focus on my job. I am one of those people that when I am upset or stressed I throw myself into my work, it gives me solace and a sense of control.

For many years, I was very comfortable working in the city's financial sector.

Then something in me just snapped and one day I decided that I needed a change. I felt that over the years I became married to my job and needed peace of mind. So I told my parents I was leaving my job in banking to pursue a career in the media – which literally went down like a nuclear bomb. After a month, I found a job in a media company and truthfully I was left genuinely tired from everything - work, the rishtas, men and generally just the daily grind.

I needed a break from any form of aggro. Admittedly the money in media is not that great when you are starting out, but I thought that at least I would be able to spend more time with my family and friends and do a job that I actually enjoyed rather than do a job simply to pay for three luxurious holidays a year, expensive nights out and lavish gifts for myself.

Thanks to a recommendation by a really good friend of mine, I started working for a media company. It was a new and fresh start for me. I got on with my boss and my colleagues seemed really nice.

I was bringing new ideas to the channel and then I met Ronnie.

Now Ronnie was the Deputy Manager of the company and he had been in the company a lot longer than me. He commanded a lot of respect amongst our colleagues. He was not gob smackingly attractive but he did have a certain attraction about him. He was full on energy, tall, well-built (not clinically obese or anything), a chain-smoker, seemed full of beans and had a GSOH (Always a great quality to have).

It was a long time since I met someone with so much energy and pizzazz. For a few weeks he helped me train up for the job that I would be doing and was really supportive when I made errors.

After a couple of weeks I had completed my training and was ready to fly solo. I started to work really odd hours and Ronnie would often come and give me company. He would bring me curly fries from the local chicken shop or what I called 'the sweaty chicken shop. He would send me Blackberry messages to keep me awake and show up during my shift to give me company at work.

Just before Christmas we had all been asked to take part in a publicity event near Brent cross, which is not very far from where I live. I had gone to bed really late and explained to my boss that I would arrive after midday. Ronnie being the most tech-savvy guy within the company, had to be there from the crack of dawn to set up. But as soon as I got up out of bed, I saw that there was about a foot of snow outside.

I called Ronnie and asked 'So what's the plan?' to which he replied 'I'm packing up, as the snow is getting heavier and the event has been called off.' He told me that he was starving and since I hadn't eaten I said 'Why don't you come to my area? As I haven't eaten we can go somewhere local.' Within an hour, Ronnie showed up. We went to a local restaurant and had some food. For some reason, I thought Ronnie was married. He never said anything and I never asked, but he just had that 'I'm married' kind of look about him. After sitting down and tucking into a meat feast, he told me he had a dilemma - he said 'I've been seeing this girl, but I really don't feel like it's going anywhere. I've recently met this other girl and I really like her - she's funny, attractive, intelligent and I can see myself having a future with her - what should I do?'

Being completely oblivious to the whole situation, I told him "It's not fair to be with someone you don't really care about. You should be with someone who you really like and you can keep happy." He then asked me 'How come you are single?' I gave him a brief summary of the last few chapters and he just laughed. I explained that I was looking for a nice guy who would love me and make me the centre of his world by giving me his time, treat me with respect and dignity - not just use and abuse me.

After food we went back to my house and on the way down were slipping and sliding down the hill. A poor Asian woman in a burka on the opposite side of the road decided to wear heels and kept falling on her backside every ten seconds. At first we found it hilarious then we started to feel really bad for the poor woman.

We got back to my house and started to watch the Million Pound Drop Live with Davina McCall.

I loved the show and really got into it. Whilst watching the show Ronnie told me that he really cared about me, to which I responded with a very nice and cordial 'Awww that's so sweet of you, I care about you too' (in a matey matey kind of way). I honestly had no idea about his feelings so carried on watching the telly.

After he left, he sang a song for me and sent it to me on my Blackberry messenger. It was a beautiful Bollywood song called 'You have no idea how much I love you.' At that point I realised what the entire conversation earlier meant and knew at this point we needed to talk.

A couple of days went by and my family came to see me Ronnie had some events, but we stayed in touch. We met up and went out for dinner. After dinner, he dropped me home and afterwards I invited him in and said, 'look Ronnie I think you are a wonderful guy but I've been through a lot recently and am really not looking for a relationship (WITH ANYONE). I'm sure I'll be ready at some point but I don't feel comfortable being with someone who is still in a semi-relationship and someone who I work with." He assured me that he had ended it with the woman he was seeing and she clearly liked him a lot, but he was really over it.

The thing is, even though I liked Ronnie, I really wasn't mentally ready to date him. I had had a rough few months with my previous job and had began suffering from severe insomnia, to the point that my poor Doctor had no idea what to do with me. So for New Years, I decided I needed a change of scenery from London and got ready to go and party with some friends in Glasgow.

Whilst in Scotland, I planned on attending the Ice Ball with some friends to bring the in the New Year. When I was up there I told my friends about Ronnie and they were really supportive. I spoke to my best friend Jag and he was brilliant. He said that 'You've been through a lot recently and you will know if you are ready or not. But I'm sure that whatever you do you'll make the right choice. Just don't rush into anything that you will regret."

I then partied with my friends for three days with literally five hours sleep, as if it was literally 1999. Whilst in Glasgow - or 'Glasvegas'as I like to call it - I was getting non-stop messages from Ronnie, who had to work over the new year weekend. When I got back to London I put my phone on silent and literally fell asleep. What I didn't realise was the fact that I had slept for 42 hours and had only two hours to get ready to get to work. When I looked at my phone I saw ten missed calls, four text messages and a few blackberry messages from Ronnie. It was at that moment that I realised that I liked him.

I messaged him straight back and went to work. The very next day Ronnie came to see me after work. We sat down and started talking. I explained that I really feared having my heart broken, I explained that I did not believe in sex before marriage and he seemed fine with it. So from that moment I realised that even though Ronnie was from a different religion to me, maybe this could work?

Over the next few weeks Ronnie and I started to hang out even more. We would go to the cinema, go for dinner, he even took me bowling, which was hilarious. I thought I had met someone who treated me with respect and dignity. Once we went out to Nandos and as we had literally got into the car park, Ronnie got a call from home. He put the phone to my ear, started laughing and said "listen to this". What I then heard was his father bawling with tears down the phone screaming "Why have you left me? Where are you? I'm at home and I want to know where you are? When will you be home? I want you here!" I was in shock and could not believe what I had heard. I immediately told Ronnie to go home to his father, but he was hungry and wanted to eat. I could not swallow a bite after hearing that. After we finished, Ronnie dropped me home.

When he dropped me, and got home himself he called to tell me "You'll never guess what I just got home and my dad is sound asleep." I was livid. As this had not only put a complete downer on the evening and my mood, but was such a pointless activity that I could not believe what had just happened.

Nevertheless I let it slide and put it down to his father's insecurity and protectiveness.

Ronnie came from a broken home, his mother left him when he was a child, and had passed away a few years later. So his father had raised him by himself, playing the part of both parents. Ronnie said that for a long time he felt a duty to his father and knew that once he settled down he would have to move out of his dad's house and live by himself and start his own family. In my mind I thought - this guy is mature, level-headed and understood the career choice I had made. He knew family values and would be someone I could see with me long-term.

I have relatives of my own who have had to deal with domestic abuse, broken homes and divorce, so I knew what he had gone through and some of the hardship he had endured and I vowed from that moment forward that I would always make him feel loved and accepted at mine.

Over the following months we became a lot stronger. We would talk about things, discuss the future and more importantly how we would speak to my parents about this.

Being an Asian, there are three things every Asian parent dreads:

1) Mum and Dad I have failed my exams.

2) Mum and Dad I'm pregnant (if you're not married-this can result in a stroke/heart failure/beating for you or any other act of violence).

3) Mum and Dad here is your future son in law.

In this case my worry was the third.

I was seriously concerned, not because of Ronnie's background or looks, my parents are very open minded and liberal when it comes to life choices. My worry was timing. My dad is a politician and as an elected politician his preparation for the elections starts well before the date is even announced. Our house becomes an election zone. We are supposed to eat, sleep, drink and breathe lections. Time off is taken from work so I can campaign, leaflet, get my hands bitten off by people's dogs and do anything I can to help me Dad keep his seat. This election was more a matter of pride for our family than anything else, so I tried to explain this to Ronnie. That's why I made the conscious decision to wait until the elections were over to introduce Ronnie and tell my family about him.

I met with Ronnie's father and we got on quite well (so I thought).I went to his place, as he felt it was important for his dad to get on with his girl. I visited his dad, making sure I never neglected him whenever Ronnie and I were planning on going out. Ronnie's father was quite a plump, fair, dark-haired uncle who had a speech problem, whereby he would mispronounce certain things such as say 'him' instead of 'her'. However his mental senses were perfectly intact. He suffered from high blood pressure, arthritis and diabetes, which are all very common Asian illnesses these days. He was very lucky because his family lived close by and would support him with his day-to-day activities. A few months after we dated, Ronnie's dad got a chest infection and was taken to hospital. Ronnie was a state - he could not come into work. Being as supportive as I could I went to see him in the Hospital. Now I live in North London and Ronnie lives in the heart of South London or "saaaaf Landaaan", as he liked to call it. I have no idea why? But people from South and East London have this obsession with hyping up their neck of the woods. I am from the North and I swear we don't do that!

Anyway jokes aside...So every day I was making the journey from North to South, helping my dad out in Wales with his election campaign and doing my domestic chores in between. Ronnie's relatives had come from India and they were a true delight. They were so sweet and even made dinner for me and invited me round. We talked about everything from films to politics, to religion as well as general chit-chat. They were genuinely lovely and we got on like a house on fire.

A few weeks later they left when Ronnie's Dad started to feel better. I went to see how he was doing. We were on our way out when he turned to me when Ronnie was changing his shoes and said 'Nikki, can you go in the cupboard under the stairs, get a duster and clean my blinds.' I'm not going to lie I was stunned.

Firstly why would you ask someone to do that when they are not even part of your family? Thankfully at that exact moment my cousin called me, so I ignored it and took the call in Ronnie's kitchen. But I was appalled and began to wonder, is that all Ronnie's Dad wanted? Someone who would be a domestic cleaner for him and for Ronnie?

I then started to get ready to go back to Wales for the election. I must admit, after this incident my worry levels were on the increase. Lots of little things had happened that had me concerned about the relationship. Now I'm quite a verbal person, but when I have to talk about some serious matters I occasionally forget certain points and get stressed. So I wrote Ronnie a letter. It was the hardest thing I ever had to do. I knew he would be angry and annoyed with me, and mentally I was prepared that this letter would result in the end of our friendship. The letter was four pages long. I expressed that I cared a lot, however I was concerned about some of the things his father had said to me. Ronnie and I had a row a few weeks before and as most people do, we shouted and screamed, got a bit weepy over it. However when I went to Ronnie's after we called it a truce, his father said '*Nikki, I never listen to Ronnie's conversations, but today when I got out of bed I listened to what you said to him through the door and you made him cry.*'

I was beyond furious. Understanding aside, I know that when you live with family, conversations are heard. But then to say something like that when Ronnie was not there was a very unpleasant experience, and one when I asked him about he called me *'a liar'* something I refuse to be called and left me seething.

The election was hugely stressful and it was a nail-biting time as my father was only given a five per cent chance of winning and, being politics, there were many people vying for his position and the opportunity to put him down (believe me anyone who thinks politics is easy needs to have a LONG conversation with me - I will happily give you a reality check). Thankfully my dad won the election and it was nail biting - not just for the results also regarding the consequences of the letter I had written to Ronnie expressing my feelings. Being away for three weeks I felt awful. Ronnie kept messaging me saying that he needed to talk and part of me really wanted to know if this was worth it or not?

So I went back to London for a weekend, when I was back Ronnie and I met up and sat down and discussed the letter, he assured me that he did not want another carer for his father, He wanted a wife who he could have his own life with. One thing I adored about Ronnie was his honesty and openness. When we first met he explained that his previous relationships had ended due to his dad and he was determined not to let it happen again. We agreed to put the letter behind us and move forward. We then had a wonderful time. I decided to treat Ronnie to a day out - we went to Edgware road, stuffed our faces with Shwarmas, went shopping through Oxford street (heaven for me), then we went to the Ice Bar just off Oxford circus. Ronnie had never been and I thought as I had been away for three weeks and was aware that if the shoe was on the other foot, I would be feeling pretty neglected. Hence I was determined to ensure that Ronnie at no point was made to feel that I did not care, as that was simply not true.

Like most people, Ronnie and I had our ups and downs. He was fiercely jealous whenever I would give another guy attention of any sort and spent a lot of time having to reassure him that I was not interested in them. We had an enormous row when a guy I worked with asked me out. I am not the cheating type and was not interested at all. Now I am a huge believer in being honest and that's how I have always been with family and friends. But that soon changed when I told Ronnie what happened, he swore, cursed and would made snippy comments about this guy Aman we worked with, saying *"He's a player, he's got a lot of girls on the go, Aman was seeing another girl that we worked with called Richa"* who also had an enormous crush on Ronnie and made life very difficult for us, by sending me random messages, 'wishing us a great relationship' and other sarcastic comments which made me feel pretty uneasy. Ronnie reassured me and I was fine, but when the tables were turned, he was not reassured at all or even seemed trusting at times.

We had been up for more than forty hours on the night of the election. My parents and I were utterly zombified. We were beyond comprehension as my father had just experienced an amazing victory not just on a personal but a professional level too.

As soon as the results were announced at six in the morning, we went home, got showered, had our breakfast then headed off to the Welsh Assembly to have him oathed in. Believe me it was like one sense of relief was over and I was petrified to say anything to him about Ronnie. After Dad was oathed in at Cardiff Bay we were shown his new office. Afterwards, we went into Cardiff town centre. As I was starving, we decided to go to Tiger Tiger to have some small snacks. When we sat down, we were talking about everything about the election and what the plan of action was. As we all raised our glasses for the victory toast. I turned to my dad and said 'Dad I have something to tell you...I have met someone, his name is Ronnie, we work together and he would like to meet you and Mum." To my shock and surprise, my father turned around and said *"WHAT!! You tell me this after the toast? We should have toasted this good news.'* I was so relieved, although his concern was that Ronnie was Sikh and being Muslims how would we adjust. I had sat Ronnie down months ago and explained that I want to have a Nikkah (a Muslim form of marital vows) and Ronnie had agreed to it. He was worried that I would want or expect him to become a very conservative Muslim, but I am not completely insolent and understand that even though Ronnie and his father were not religious at all. I was sure that he would want to make 'our children' - if we ever were to have any - aware of his faith and traditions. Which I never had or would object to.

My father seemed pleased that Ronnie would accept my religion and agreed to meet him, so he agreed to invite Ronnie to our house in Wales after two weeks.

I was so happy to get back to London after the election. It's a draining and stressful time for everyone involved and I actually was missing work. So I could not wait to get back to London. When I did, I spoke to Ronnie and told him about my parents' reaction. We arranged that he would come back to Wales with me after two weeks to meet my family. I could tell that in the run up to their first meeting, Ronnie was really nervous. He was thinking about everything - possible questions they would ask, what to wear, what to say. You name it he was worried about it, which was really sweet as I could tell he wanted to make a good impression. Around the same time Ronnie started to have car problems. He drove a bright red Toyota, which I called his *'Love wagon'* (no dirty pun intended). It was summer time and for some reason the car would keep over-heating, so whenever Ronnie and I would go out it would be twenty four/five degrees and we would have to put the radiators on to ensure the car didn't over heat. We decided that it would be viable if we took my car home to my parents. When I arrived at Ronnie's house on Saturday he was all over the place. The poor guy couldn't decide if he should wear a three-piece or a two-piece suit. Now I love a man in a suit, but I knew that his nervousness plus a three hour drive to Wales would be made a lot easier if Ronnie wore a pair of smart jeans, black shoes, a waistcoat and pinstripe jacket. He looked smart and casual. Before we left for Wales, we had to do a mad dash to Tesco as he wanted to pick up a plant for my mum and some sweets for the journey, which was very charming and really sweet on his part.

We eventually got to Wales and he was greeted by both of my parents, we sat down in the living room. Did the whole samosa, soft drink, tea/coffee soiree as per routine but it was a lot more chilled than before. My parents asked about Ronnie's, job, his dad, future goals and ambitions and they seemed to get on really well. However I could tell my mum was not one hundred per cent confident about him as Ronnie had not obtained a degree. Not having a degree is a really big NO NO for my mum.

Ronnie told my parents that when he went to University to study Medicine his father became very sick, this kept happening eventually, Ronnie had to drop out and go home to be with his dad. My parents understood family values and thought if Ronnie is such a considerate man he'll surely take care of me too.

After dinner I popped upstairs to get a cardigan for myself and my mum and Ronnie were on the dining table he sat next to my mum and said "*Aunty I really love Nikki. She means the world to me and I promise that I will never break her heart. I will never let her or you down and I will make sure everything she wants in life is fulfilled.*" My mum was heart strings had been yanked well and good. They only thing my parents did not like was his addiction to smoking.

Being very health conscious, both of my parents are against smoking and did not want Ronnie to ruin his health. My father even gave Ronnie a lighter as a gift in the hope he would slowly quit the habit. Ronnie and I then made our way back to London. His dad wanted to know how everything went and seemed content that the first meeting had gone well.

A few weeks after Ronnie came to my house, he and his father invited my parents to his house. My mum and dad drove to London the night before and got all ready for the lunch at Ronnie's house on Sunday. I was told by my mum to doll up in a traditional Punjabi suit, which was hilarious as Ronnie had never seen me in one. Before we left, Ronnie called me and said "*Please try and take your time as I'm still waiting for the food to be ready.*"

Which made me laugh as Ronnie was never able to be on time - something that drove me bonkers since I am a self-confessed OCD when it comes to time-keeping. For many years I've had the innate habit of being early for everything. I despise being late. I would rather be fifteen minutes early than even a minute late. For being on time shows respect for another person's time, for each person their time is precious and it's not something that I want to waste, so I expect the same respect back.

Anyway, my OCD habits aside, I navigated my parents to Ronnie's house. When we arrived at his house, a modest terrace in South London based in a predominant Asian area, Ronnie and his dad had always lived in the same house. His father had gone through a lot of hardship when he was younger, and I can respect that. He worked to make life better for Ronnie. Though Ronnie always had a lot of respect for his dad, looking back now at times it seemed a little un-healthy.

My parents and I entered the house to be welcomed by Ronnie. We went into the living room to be greeted by Ronnie's father and his housekeeper Rita, who came every Sunday to keep the house clean. Rita was in her late fifties, plump, fair, had gorgeous long hair like Kim Kardashian, lived locally and was very sweet. She would occasionally cook for Ronnie's father, give him some adult conversation and attention, administered his medication, which he needed and craved as he did not really have any friends or even left the house very much. We sat down and Rita bought in glasses of orange juice for us. My dad, being the king of conversations started chatting away to his father and I went into the kitchen to help Ronnie. He and his dad had truly made an impressive selection of food. Which made me think 'wow they really want this to work.'

They had made a number of curries and dishes, which my parents loved. I could tell that Ronnie was nervous as he wanted to make a good impression, Rita eventually left after making small talk. Then we proceeded to the kitchen to eat, the food was delicious and we were impressed. I helped Ronnie with the dishes afterwards and we sat down in the living room. The topic moved to music, Ronnie's forte, and he quickly even made a CD for my mum with some old school Bollywood tracks - something he'd never done for me! But I was sincerely touched by the gesture and so was my mother. After a few hours someone from Social Services came to take one of his father's Zimmer frames away and his father got into a panic when he realised they had taken the wrong one. Ronnie took him aside and said *"Dad calm down, stay calm, I'll sort it out, we have guests right now - don't ruin this for me'.'* Ronnie's father continued on shouting but he calmed down eventually.

We were a tad surprised by the outburst but carried on with the afternoon. We then met Ronnie's father's carer Connie, a heavily pregnant Bengali woman who visited the house daily to make sure Ronnie's father took his medication, that he was dressed, fed and his sugar levels were ok.

I was glad that Ronnie's father had carers to make sure his health was in check. I've dealt with a sick parent from a young age - my mother suffered from a condition of Fibromyalgia (Chronic Fatigue Syndrome) and was a cancer patient. We never had any carers in the house, thankfully she overcame it and does occasionally have the odd bad day) so believe me when

I say, I know it does take its toll on loved ones. However, I'm not very hard-core and cannot stand the sight of blood, injections or vomit. Connie was very sweet and made very nice chit-chat with my parents. Whilst Connie was chatting to my parents and Ronnie gave them a guided tour of the house, Ronnie's father pulled me aside and said 'Nikki, I want to tell your parents about Ronnie's exes, they should know about everything." Now I'm all for being honest, however I could not understand Ronnie's father's desire to tell my parents about his relationships past, as nothing was going on with any of his exes. It just seemed a futile exercise that would be helpful if one was trying to burn bridges, not make them. I didn't say anything and told Ronnie's father *"It's irrelevant and that's not what they need to hear."* It eventually took Ronnie losing his temper with him to get the message across and stop touting this topic of conversation every five minutes.

The lunch at Ronnie's went very well. It resulted in my parents inviting Ronnie and his father to

Wales, but I could tell that my mother still had some doubts. Her doubtful facial expression said it all.

When we all went and sat with Ronnie and his father after the slap-up meal they had made, my mother asked, 'So where are you (Ronnie) and Nikki going to live?' To which Ronnie replied, "We're going to move in with Dad and live here.' I was a tad taken aback, Ronnie and I had discussed this, but his sudden outburst had left me speechless.

Now I have no qualms about living with my in-laws. In fact I knew it is part of our culture to move in with our in-laws for a bit and then move into our own place. However, when Ronnie proceeded to say to my parents *I'm thinking about getting a six bedroom place and get Dad to live in the annex*, I was bewildered. I sat there thinking this guy does not have the bank balance of Bill Gates yet he somehow thinks that he can conjure a six bedroom house in London and his father will live with the annex. I had no animosity with Ronnie's father, but over the last few times I had been to his house I had noticed certain things.

Ronnie's father had renovated the living room and had made it quite a little bachelor pad for himself. He got Ronnie to pick out a widescreen TV with all the 4D trimmings. His father sat on what I had named the throne, the only single chair in the room next to the door, in perfect line with the TV and all other amenities. However Ronnie never once sat and watched TV, because his father would always be watching his usual Asian channels. In fact Ronnie would go to his room to watch freeview when he needed space. Not once had I seen Ronnie's father give him the remote control and say '*Here son, you put on whatever you like.*' It was summertime and one day Ronnie decided to take his shirt off, he was fully clothed (don't get the wrong impression) however his father screamed '*PUT YOUR SHIRT BACK ON! WHAT ARE YOU DOING?*' I was once again left speechless. Don't get me wrong, I have no intention of walking around my house topless. However when someone gets married, surely they should be able to do what they like in the privacy of their own home? I could see that element of privacy diminish each time his father made an abrupt comment or was around. When I spoke to Ronnie about it, I must admit I was scared to talk to him because I knew how sensitive he was about his father - he felt responsible for his mother abandoning them and often bought it up when he was feeling low, so I would do everything to assure him that I would stand by him and take on the world with him and for him. Oddly he never said anything remotely similar to me.

His father became a very sensitive subject between us and it was starting to get me down whenever I would talk to Ronnie about anything his father had said. He would call me a 'liar' and say 'my father is a saint, you don't know what you're talking about!' So I took the oath of silence and chose to keep quiet, as it wasn't worth the hassle and Ronnie had this disgusting habit that if you ever spoke to him about a topic he knew was touchy such as his dad, he would somehow bring his mother's abandonment issues into it and blame her for making him responsible for his father. He would generally blame her absence for his short comings and the reason for his bad behaviour.

After our visit to Ronnie's house for lunch, my family thought it would only seem appropriate if we invited Ronnie and his father to ours for dinner and to stay with us.

It would be a good opportunity for my parents to find out what Ronnie and his father wanted and foresaw as our future together. My mother was always sceptical of him and his '*intentions*' as she believed that all he wanted was a woman to take care of his father so he could go out with peace of mind, finally focus on his career, and leave me at home to make food and take care of the children. As Ronnie assured me after the letter (I had written months ago) this would not be the case.

Truthfully I was rather surprised by Ronnie's sudden outburst when my parents simply asked about our living arrangements. So before he came to my house I asked him outright 'What had changed?' To which he said 'I cannot leave my dad. Wherever we go, Dad will come with us.' In the past, his father had always said with a goofy smile 'You two go and be happy, get your own house and come and see me.' Little did I know that this was Ronnie's father's way of guilt-tripping him in, the psychological warfare they both play with each other.

After hearing his father say that, Ronnie screamed 'Dad you will live with us, did you get that?! I am not leaving you,' My initial reaction was 'whaaaaaaaat?' but I thought maybe because they were scarred by his mother leaving them both, this was just a backlash to that. Then I thought, hang on we've all had bad stuff happen to us in life, it shouldn't be the bearing on holding us down from bettering ourselves? But that was a view that Ronnie never took. His *woe to me* attitude really started to get me down. Whenever I would talk to him about "our" future, "our" living arrangements "our" life, he would dodge the subject or make it all about his father. So I thought the best thing to do would be maintain silence and see what happened.

A couple of weeks after our trip to the South of London, Ronnie and his father came to Wales. I had driven home the night before to help my mum out with any work that needed to be done. We made the usual samosas, chickpea chaat, lamb curry, chicken curry, a few vegetarian dishes and chapattis,

They arrived on time, being a few hours late due to their being a rugby match in the Millennium stadium. When they arrived they were received by all three of us, standing in the reception like the Queen's Guard.

Once they arrived we sat down and made small talk about the journey, work, his father's health, and the usual general topics of conversation.

Afterwards I served everyone tea and offered the usual savouries. The doorbell rang and my grandfather was there on the doorstep. Now my grandfather is a sweetheart. He was always eloquent, had an accent that would rival a Royal and was always immaculately dressed. That day, my Nana looked like he'd just come back from umpiring a cricket match. All in white and cream, with a sun hat and sun glasses, shoes polished to perfection. My grandfather lives two streets away from my parents' house and is regarded as the elder of the family. He's in his mid-eighties and has been all over the world. When it comes to marriages, he 'interviews' new entrants into our family and ensures that potential suitors are up to scratch. I remember when my aunt was being introduced to potential suitors he made one guy actually faint, because his interviewing nature is a force to be reckoned with.

My father explained that Ronnie was a potential suitor for me. As my grandfather was hard of hearing and refuses to wear a hearing aid, we had to shout everything. Ronnie was clearly nervous and scooted his chair next to my grandfather. My grandfather asked him 'What do you do? Where do you live? What are your future aspirations?' The usual kind of questions. But to our surprise, every time Ronnie would answer a question his father would butt in with 'tell him Ronnie, tell him about me..Tell him Ronnie, tell him what I used to do.' A little bit surprising to us all, as it was Ronnie potentially getting married not his father.

Anyway, after chatting to Ronnie for a while my grandfather put his thumbs up which was always considered a good sign.

We then conjoined for dinner. Whilst sitting down for food, my dad tends to offer food to the younger generation first. My mum poured food for my grandfather and everyone else was fairly self-sufficient. All of a sudden came this voice ''Papa can I pour you some food? Papa would you like some pani (water)? Papa would you like lamb or chicken? Ronnie was babysitting his dad in front of all of us, and I was truly dumbstruck - I'm talking jaw-on-the-ground and eyes-popping-out-of-my-head like a

Warner Brothers Cartoon. He then poured food for himself and he and his papa started eating with the rest of the family. I was shocked. Where did this mothering Ronnie come from? Where did this 'Papa' business come from? What happened to the normal 'Dad'?

I understand that meeting a girl's family can be nerve wracking, But to have a personality transplant in the space of a couple of days was shocking! Not once did Ronnie offer me any food and I was more than unamused, it was something my grandfather and even had to ask my mother about it later on.

After dinner was over, my grandfather needed to take his medication so he left. Ronnie, his father, my mum and dad were sitting at the table. I went upstairs to get changed. When I returned they all sent me to the front room as they wanted to have a 'private conversation'. I assumed that they were doing something about my birthday so I went into the front room and started to watch Die Hard.

After about half an hour, Ronnie's father needed to change his clothes so I offered to help him. I have elderly relatives and know some need help with their shoes, buttons, coats so totally understand. We went upstairs. Ronnie was busy chatting away to my parents downstairs. By the time we came downstairs, Ronnie was gagging for a cigarette so we went for a walk and left our parents to it. When we returned, my dad was being really strange with me. I asked if he was okay? To which he replied 'yes, I'm fine.'

A week after they left my father had been really odd with me. We went on a shopping trip for Ronnie's birthday gift to Westfield. After getting some really lovely outfits for him, we got back in the car and my dad turned and said 'Nikki are you and Ronnie having sex?' I swear I nearly died. For an Asian girl/woman to be asked that by her father is so unbelievably shameful and embarrassing. Let me put it like this if someone gave me the option of being asked that or being stabbed, I would choose the latter.

I looked at my dad stunned as a rabbit before the headlights and said 'where on earth did you get that from?' He went quiet and said 'Ronnie's Dad.' I said 'What the hell did he say?' To which my dad replied when Ronnie and I had gone out during their most recent visit to our house, his father had gone and sat down with my parents to watch TV. He then turned to my dad during the News and said 'I really like it when Nikki comes and sees me and Ronnie.' Knowing my dad when the news is on, it's hard enough to get conversation out of him let alone a reaction. So my dad said 'That's nice.' When Ronnie's father saw this had no effect Ronnie's father said 'I like it a lot when Nikki comes and spends time with us.' Once again my father gave a (I'm not bothered look) and his usual comment of 'that's nice.' This is when Ronnie's dad went in for the kill. 'I really like it when Nikki sleeps in Ronnie's bed.' - I was mortified.

Only God, my mother and my father know how much it took for me to convince my dad that there was no hanky panky going on. My mother had a feeling that Ronnie's father was being sweet as pie towards me in public however secretly despised me, for ripping his son away from his womb. I had always treated Ronnie's father with respect acknowledging him, giving him a Father's Day gift, birthday, everything. I knew he would probably feel insecure and always reassured him that I would want to rip away his son. However it was clear from that moment onwards, disabled or not Ronnie's father was on a mission to break us up.

Over time Ronnie and I became quite close. He always said that he never liked to have a big birthday. Now I love my birthday, it is perhaps the one day of the year where I get to celebrate, party, let my hair down and enjoy my day. However Ronnie was not of the same belief. He did not 'big up' his own birthday. He liked to traditionally spend his day with his dad at home. I thought since he was going to be my fiancée and the meeting with my parents had gone so well, I would organise a surprise birthday for him. So I contacted his friends and asked them to put the word out. Now as I mentioned before, the media industry doesn't pay a lot money and Ronnie was beginning to get successful and recognised by a lot of artists. So upon his constant reminder about what he thought of birthdays, I thought a close family affair would be fine. I spoke to Ronnie's father and made the plan clear. I would sort out all the nibbles and drinks, and we would order pizza from outside. Ronnie's Dad said 'Nikki, I won't be able to do much but I insist on paying for the pizza' which was fine with me.

The party would be at home with all of his close friends in attendance, I would make bits and pieces and his dad would pay for the pizza when it was delivered.

Ronnie and I had gone shopping a few months ago and he told me that he would know that he had 'made it big in life' if he got a Breitling watch. I worked like a woman possessed doing as many TV shows, radio shows, taking on media projects as I could often working eighteen hour days to make sure I could afford his gifts, drinks and food.

A couple of days before his birthday, Ronnie had been asked to attend an event the same day as his birthday. He agreed to do it and knowing Ronnie, who is never on time, I thought - Oh goodness, he'll miss his own birthday when he's taking his time going from one venue to the other! So I had to drop enough hints and tell him that there would be a small shin dig at his house, for his birthday.

My parents are amazing and have always said if I ever need money for anything I can access their bank accounts. However, I wanted to bear the expense for this myself. I really liked Ronnie and wanted to prove to myself that I could afford this birthday myself. In between working long days the night before his birthday I had gone on a shoot to Wimbledon on my way back to the car I slipped in the road and gashed both of my knees really badly. Then I went home to clean up and leave again to go for a birthday meal arranged by his friends near central London, I then left early to head off to work to finish a project I was working on which finished at 1am.Then I went home and stood over the stove and made over one hundred onion bajis. God bless twenty four hour superstores where I was able to go and pick up samosas to fry the next day, I was able to get drinks, paper plates, cups, glasses you name it, and it was there. Ronnie's friends even had children and I made sure that goodie bags were ready for them too.

The next day I flew to Ronnie's house, I wanted to be the first person to wish him 'Happy birthday' when he woke up. I gave him his birthday gifts which consisted of the Breitling, a new outfit, a phone cover and lots of other little bits and bobs, including my parents' gift for him.

I must admit something felt a bit funny when I gave Ronnie the watch. He seemed least bothered. In fact it seemed like he was finding it hard to even say thank you. Instead he turned around and said, 'Babe, you know I said to your parents that I would propose to you on your birthday?' I replied with a confused 'yes' he then turned around and said 'Well, I don't think I can, as I can't afford the ring.' I was stunned and very disappointed. However, as it was his birthday, I thought it would be best to carry on with the day.

I went to his kitchen, started making a dish called *dahi bareh* (an indian savoury dish that consists of onion bajis in yoghurt with lots of spices.) I made two enormous trays of them and got them ready for Ronnie's friend's arrival. When his friends came they all jokingly cussed me for not keeping the party a secret, when I told them that if I didn't tell him, he would probably not have been back until the middle of the night. So all was forgiven and the party began.

It is also worth mentioning that Ronnie's birthday fell upon a traditional festival called *Karva chauth* (a day where a woman fasts the whole day for her husband or husband-to-be and prays for his long life. It can be done by married and single women) Since things were going so well between us (or so I thought) I decided to keep a fast for Ronnie. That whole day Ronnie's Dad kept saying on and on and on '*Nikki, why are you fasting it's not Karva chauth today!*' I admit it started to get on my nerves I told Ronnie to look at his Twitter and Facebook as everyone under the sun was gearing up for it and wishing others the best for their fast. Eventually he went and told his dad 'It's Karva chauth today, leave her alone.' Finally his father stopped going on about it and accepted that I was right, but kept saying "*Nikki, make me tea, give me some of the onion baji's, I want some deyh bareh that you've made.*"

I thought Ronnie's Dad is not very well so fair enough, but Ronnie is at least kind and considerate towards me. But that day Ronnie changed. He was stuffing his face in front of me with food. I did not expect him to starve himself but I did expect him to be a tad more understanding considering this is something that isn't part of my religion or culture?!

When his friends arrived, he was showing his friends all of the gifts he had received from colleagues and friends, but no mention about anything I had given him. It was insulting quite frankly and hurt my feelings. His friends arrived one by one. It was a pretty male-dominated environment, but I had met most of his friends beforehand, and they were very welcoming. I was in the kitchen frying up the samosas and sorting out the food.

A lot of his friends stayed with me in the kitchen to keep me company. Some were in the garden, and some were in Ronnie's studio - a small conservatory linked to the kitchen where he was banging out some of his music. Halfway through the evening, his father came into the kitchen and said 'Nikki, why has everyone left me? Why are you all in the kitchen? Why don't you all come and sit with me in the living room?' I was quite surprised by this little outburst, Ronnie's friends felt uncomfortable and as Ronnie was too busy mingling with his friends, he didn't seem too bothered so some of his friends took it in shifts to sit with his father one by one. Whilst they were in there, quite a few came in and said "Nikki, Ronnie's Dad wants food, tea, biscuits" and lots of other bits and pieces, which was dutifully sent out to him.

As the night progressed, Ronnie invited some new colleagues to our office. When they arrived they came and mingled with me and his other friends, then all of a sudden said "Come on! You all must come and meet Dad" One of the girls faces looked horrified, but they all went in and said "Hello". After a few hours, the party got rowdy and people were getting hungry. Ronnie called up for pizzas. When they arrived, one of his friends tapped me on the shoulder and said "Nikki, the pizza guy is here and wants seventy pounds." I told his friend Jit that "Ronnie's Dad would be paying for it". He disappeared for five minutes and came back saying "Ronnie's Dad has gone AWOL".

I was un-amused, annoyed and livid. Firstly he had said he would deal with the responsibility of the food. Now it had arrived he was nowhere to be seen. He had not at any point helped or offered to help, just said 'I wish I could help you Nikki,'. He had not even bought a birthday card for his son, I had to get it. Nor had he even bothered with a gift. That wasn't my problem or concern, but I was tired, annoyed and now irritated to top it off. Ronnie was behaving oddly. I then ran around the house looking for Ronnie's father who had locked himself into the bathroom conveniently for half an hour. I could not even get to my bag in Ronnie's room as his father's sport's equipment was in the way. Somehow he had decided the day the house was to be filled with people he was going to train to compete with Usain Bolt in the next Olympics.

When I got downstairs I saw Ronnie's friends pooling their money together to pay for the food. At this point I felt utterly humiliated and even apologised for something that was not even my responsibility.

As it was karva chauth, once the moon came up it was time to eat for me, so having fed the entire party, I was the only one who hadn't eaten anything. For some reason the moon was taking forever to come up, Ronnie's father kept screaming every two minutes 'Isn't the moon out yet?" which if you are hungry as it is and cannot see the blooming moon is the last thing you want to hear. Anyway Ronnie was in the street waiting for a friend from the music industry. I was in the kitchen frying some samosas when his friend CJ came in and said 'Nikki do you know the moon is out?' I asked 'Where's Ronnie?' His friend CJ said he's outside, as he was forming a welcome committee for his friend. I went outside only to hear his father scream 'IS THE MOON OUT YET?' I said a small prayer for him in Arabic. He gave me some food and water. Once that was done, I said 'So Ronnie where is my award for keeping a fast?' Ronnie then went into his wallet pulled out his debit card in front of his friends and rammed it down my top and said 'Here's your gift.' I was mortified. I was so angry and wanted to call a cab and go home. He then followed me inside and said 'I need my card back' I swear, if it wasn't his birthday I would have cut his card into little pieces and thrown them in the bin, but I kept my cool.

It was after this point Ronnie started to behave like a moron, he was so busy being the centre of attention he started to behave in a very rude manner towards me. When the food was being served I asked him to go and get some food. He kept saying 'No, not now, later, later' then when one of his other female friends said "Come on, let's get some food' he could not have rushed into the kitchen quicker. It was hot that evening, and when I gave him a drink he put it on the table of his studio.

Within seconds, his friend picked it up and said 'Here Ronnie have some" .Ronnie gulped it down like it was holy water.

I was upset, speechless and deeply hurt by his behaviour. I began to think, why did I bother? I don't think he even cares! Why on earth did I spend months trying to convince my folks about someone who is so rude and disrespectful towards me?

Then Ronnie's father called me into the front room and asked me to help him change his clothes. As he refused to get changed whilst a nurse was there, I was given the duty to help him change, which I didn't mind. Ronnie's father was sitting with his friend Sam, who was telling me about his life story, how he met Ronnie, as it was the first time I'd ever met him. As I was helping Ronnie's father remove his shoes. Sam started to talk to me. As soon as Ronnie's father saw my attention had been diverted to Sam he started screaming, and I don't mean a little oooh or an aaah, I mean "AAAAAAARGH!!!". I couldn't understand what happened as the first shoe and sock had come off without any issue. But Sam realised what had gone on and could see Ronnie's father was only doing it as he felt the attention on him had been diverted to me, so he apologised. Ronnie came rushing in to see what the noise was all about and Sam told him what had happened. Ronnie sat with his dad for a bit before returning to the party.

I must admit Ronnie's friends Shanway and Safi were lovely, they helped clean up and sort things out in the house. Ronnie didn't even put a glass in the sink to help. Nonetheless, it was a good party. Everyone left and Ronnie's father who is normally in bed by 11pm was up until 3am.

When the party ended, Ronnie's father sat in the front room on what I called his throne with a small brush in his hands. He looked at my face and at this point I looked as though I had been put through the mill. He said "Aww Nikki, how are your knees? Are you in pain? You must be tired?' When I said "Yes Uncle, I'm really tired and in a lot of pain, but it was worth it for Ronnie." To my horror he said "Here, take this and sweep up my floor" putting a dustpan and brush into my hands.

That was it, I had been pushed to the end of my tether by father and son. I could not believe that the son who had behaved like such an ingrate and selfish moron all night did what he did and the father had no respect or sense to say something like that to a girl his son had just told he could not get a ring for?

How much does a ring cost at Argos these days? £29.99?

After the birthday was over, I went upstairs to get my bag to be dumbstruck when I heard Ronnie belt out 'Thank you Papa for such an amazing birthday, it was amazing all because of you!!!'

I was beyond blazing with rage. I had gone to all this effort for a guy I thought cared. However the selfish oaf didn't say thank you to me but his beloved Papa who sat on his backside all night didn't lift a finger or do anything worthy of a thank you. Then two minutes later he followed me and said 'Thanks babe'. I was livid.

After Ronnie's birthday party, I was so angry and upset by his bad behaviour. Some people may think I'm being sensitive. Some may say I overreacted, but when you care about someone and they behave like an A-grade ass. There's very little you can do, after I arranged an amazing birthday and was asked by his father to get on my knees and sweep the floor which I did. I burst out into tears and as I said earlier, I despise crying in public. So I grabbed my things and headed out of the house. Ronnie flew down the stairs and followed me onto the street. He started screaming 'WHERE THE HELL ARE YOU GOING?' I just said 'I'm going home' and jumped on a bus. He continued to follow me, swear at me and scream at me in the street but I didn't care. I was beyond the point of caring and just wanted to go home and cry.

On the journey home Ronnie kept sending me texts asking if I was ok, which I clearly wasn't. I got home and as I went into my bag for my keys I realised in my quick exit I had left my house keys and coat at his house. I knocked on my next door neighbours door for ages. John is in his eighties, he lives with his son Tim and both of them are perhaps the best neighbours I have ever had, hence I trust them with my house keys. But nobody answered. Eventually, after crying on the doorstep, I got into my car and drove back to Ronnie's. Crying like a child on the way. Not knowing what I would say or do, all I wanted were my keys. When I got to Ronnie's house I buzzed the intercom and his dad answered. I flew up to Ronnie's room where he was shocked to see me. I burst out into tears and said 'I can't deal with this nonsense.I don't ever want you to choose between me and your Father, but this behaviour is ridiculous.' He asked what had happened, when I told him what his father had said and being asked to sweep up people's floor is not how you behave with your prospective daughter-in-law. He proceeded to call me 'a liar...My father would never have said that to you.' When I said 'You were sitting right there!' he lost the plot and accused me of not being understanding and unsupportive.

It was at that point something inside me snapped. I thought I had fought for this bumbling oaf, put everything I had on the line for him. Made him and his beloved Papa feel like they were 'loved', something they both apparently craved and for all my efforts I was being called a liar? Hell to the NO!

I then left Ronnie's house and went home. The next couple of days were a blur. Ronnie and I had planned that he would spend my birthday with me in

Wales and have dinner with my family. Then on Saturday we would have a party with my friends. Over the next couple of days, Ronnie sent me the most horrible text messages I have ever seen in my life. He only wished me a happy birthday on Facebook. On my birthday I waited for him to show up and apologise for his bad behaviour, but he never did. The bigger slap on my face was when I decided I'd had enough of waiting, I drove home to Wales by myself giving myself a million and one words of encouragement as I know my parents would not be happy. Whilst I was near Wales I saw his father calling on my phone only to leave me a message that was about as nice as a punch in the face. 'Helooooo Nikki, this is Ronnie's papa. I wanted to wish you a very happy birthday, happy birthday to you, happy birthday.' I was beyond devastated. The moron that I had cared about couldn't get off his backside to wish me a happy birthday, yet his troublemaking father who clearly uses his disability as an excuse to hurt others and behave badly was being as nice as pie. Clearly an act to stick the final nail in the coffin. Papa had finally got his son back.

Ronnie and I fought for weeks. He carried on sending me horrible messages and calling me to scream abuse down the phone -words like bitch, cow and other insults were quite common. I don't like swearing at others and just took it. In his finest hour he said *'I hope God puts a curse on you and may both of your parents have strokes - just so you know what it feels like. I hope God makes you barren. I hope you can never have children because you don't deserve to be a mother....I hate you...you and I can never be as I want a woman who will wipe my father's backside when he can't control himself. Will you do that?'*

I knew it would be in my best interest to keep my mouth shut, which I did. But his behaviour just got out of hand. At work he was being seen as this amazing funny, caring and kind guy. However, I was seeing a nasty piece of work who was rude, disrespectful and abusive. The worst thing was that he never once said sorry for his behaviour.

Things eventually got too much and my parents started to get worried when they saw I was constantly upset and irritated. So as a consequence I left the job I loved, more so to get away from Ronnie because it just got too much. His constant abuse, nonsense and insults became too much. Part of me always hoped that he would see sense, be a man, stop blaming his absent mother and controlling father for his bad behaviour and make amends. But the man just did not know where and when to stop. Even after I left, the nonsense continued. He told colleagues of mine that if they associated themselves with me, then he was dead to them. He showed up at a work event and started to scream at me in the street. Some of my colleagues told me afterwards that they had pre-dialled 999 on their mobiles in case he got physical. Amongst hurling abuse at me and swearing at me, he told me he 'longed for me, ached for me, wanted to be with me.' But then I got to the point where for me everything he said was just words. I just didn't believe him anymore.

At my work leaving party, he soured the mood by sending me silly messages and really upsetting me in front of my colleagues, who just couldn't understand my reasoning behind leaving. But for those people who know what being hurt is like, there comes a point where you just switch and need to breathe away from all the nonsense and mental sewage and clear your head.

Sadly Ronnie never delivered on what he said throughout the time I knew him. I kick myself for not having picked up on the warning signs but when you care, you only see the good times and good things about a person. You fail to see the manipulative and spiteful things that are right in front of you as clear as paper.

Without a doubt Ronnie said the right things and to this day can manipulate anyone with his words but sadly there is no substance. I know a lot of people lose parents, suffer illnesses, survive disasters and learn to be happy however Ronnie and his father craved attention. They claimed to want love and respect but simply didn't know how to give it back.

If there is one thing I have learnt from the Ronnie experience it is that sometimes regardless of how much you can help others, you can just not help some people enough to fill their need. There are sadly some people in this world who have been through a lot and want to better themselves after having learnt some tough life lessons. However you also get the Ronnie types who pretend they want to be happy and they want to change their circumstances. But, in actual fact they thrive on their misery and cannot fathom being away from it, because it means they will have to grow a spine and deal with the real world. Which would mean standing up on their own two feet. It takes some men a very long time to realise that happiness is right under their nose but they are so happy blaming life, their unfortunate circumstances, remaining selfish and attention-seeking to milk as much sympathy as they can from others. Sadly that is all they need to survive and thrive, not really caring or bothering with those that care about them, because heaven forbid happiness may come knocking on their door and they may have to just grow up.

As much as some guys think it, they are not Peter Pan. They all have to grow up at some point or another. Some can choose to make their life and live it to the max, others choose to sit at home with their beloved Papa's waiting for someone to come along and marry the both of them.

THE FRESHIE

I always used to say that I would **never ever** be with a guy from the homeland. (*Homeland=Indian subcontinent namely India/Pakistan*)

Now I know that sounds really racist, but I have spent a lot of time with some of my male family members of the years from the homeland. Although they are all lovely in their own ways and will make amazing dads someday, somehow they all seem to be quite self-absorbed individuals who lack in empathy. This is not only members of my own family, but also total randoms I have come across over the years and above all I find that they have a very different mind-set to people like me who are born and raised in the UK.

A few years after recovering from the trauma of finding my knight in shining armour and meeting a lot of toads along the way, I threw myself into my career and joined a hugely successful PR company. Being one of the only single women in the office, the subject of my impending marriage was a huge topic of conversation so one day my boss decided to take matters into her own hands.

The PR company that I worked for had a lot of international offices in all major countries and cities across the globe and on many occasions we had people popping in for meetings, conferences and it was during such a time that I came across a young guy called Am who was based in the New York office. He was tall, from Mumbai (not my usual type), well-dressed, very friendly and fresh as a daisy. But he did have the reputation of being the most despised man in the company, due to his cut-throat nature at work. He also had one of the strongest Indian accents I have ever heard in my life. But I liked his sense of wit and thought he was a nice guy. On a few occasions my boss attempted for us to meet by messaging me to meet her and Am for a drink. However for one reason or another I couldn't due to family or pre-planned events. We often spoke in the office and he encouraged me to write my book and ensure that it gets published, to which I just laughed and got on with my business. After a few days my boss suggested that we all go for a lunch. I was not in the mood whatsoever, but after receiving a lot of pressure from her I took him to Pizza Express - alongside six other team members. To my surprise, he very gallantly paid for the entire team's lunch, which was very sweet. Over lunch we talked about everything under the sun and after a while it became apparent that we were the only two people talking and everyone else was just sitting there, tucking into their lunches and enjoying the free show. But it was fun and we all went back to work and got on with our business.

Now I am one of those people who feels that if someone takes me out then I must repay them in some small way and in my heart knew that I would repay him back for his generosity towards myself and my team in some small way. The following day I was working late and asked him his plans for the evening and he said that he "didn't have anything major lined up." So I asked if he'd like to go for a bite to eat? I was feeling a bit under the weather and after a late work meeting we went to Westfield and ended up talking the night away. We ended the evening going for a walk around Hyde Park and it was lovely - you could call it a truly enchanting evening. We realised that we had a lot in common and when I got home at stupid o'clock, he continued to message me. He also warned me that he was a bit rubbish with communication, but ensured that I had all modes of communication such as SKYPE, Viber and all other communicative apps on my phone so he could speak to me anywhere and at any time. I thought he was really sweet and could not understand why so many people hated him at work.

A few days later he went off travelling across Europe for work and we stayed heavily in contact. During his time at my office he said how much he liked an Indian sweet called 'jalebis'. I'm not so fussed on Indian sweets, as they are a bit too sickly for me. But I kept it in mind and when he came back I had managed to lose my voice from talking to him so much, so he brought me soup to make sure I was okay. A really nice gesture that I must admit did WOW my socks off.

I am a well renowned chatterbox and it had been a long time since I had lost my voice from talking so much to someone. When he came back we did not have much time to meet as we were both working, but we decided to hang out before his flight to the Middle East on Saturday. I planned to meet him for lunch, but after not having heard from him I got a bit worried. He messaged me after lunchtime and asked if it would be okay to meet around four o'clock, which was a bit of a shocker as his flight was at eight. So I met him and we went for a quick bite to eat, in my mind I had planned a lovely day but time was a real restriction, with him having to catch a flight and I had to go to Wales for a family gathering. I offered to drive him to the airport. On our way we talked, laughed till our bellies hurt and en route I told him that there was a "small surprise" for him. He had no idea where we were, which was understandable. On our way to the airport we drove through a famous area in London known for Asian food, drinks and items known as Southall. He looked a bit baffled and when I told him that I was treating to him to jalebis as he had told me how much he loved them, he was literally speechless. He went so quiet that I didn't know what to do for a minute, but we picked the jalebis and made our way to the airport. After dropping him off he went to the Middle East, Australia, Canada and India and I have to give him full marks as he never missed my calls or missed the chance to message me. He would send me songs and some were admittedly the type that would make your heart melt. Naturally after a point I even began to miss him. As mushy as it sounds he came to the London office a few times after that but because he was always working, I hardly got a chance to see him. Many times he would message to meet late at night, which initially seemed sweet, but then became concerning. At first I felt really desired and after a point I started to feel like a bit of a time pass. I even asked him "What is this? What exactly are we to each other" to which he told me "We are exclusive". I wasn't too sure what that meant, so asked him to elaborate. He went on to tell me it meant he "would not see or be with other people" and the same rule applied to me too. I thought things were moving in the right direction and he would go ahead and say how he would take me to different places around the world (by the way, this never happened). But it sounded very nice and romantic at the time. I even spoke to some of my very dear friends about this and they all said "Nikki, take it slow. Don't go at 70MPH when you are in a 30MPH zone." All of my friends all seemed a bit confused by his nature. Even my boss was left perplexed. We all accepted that he worked long and odd hours. I suppose having a work-a-holicfather prepared me to accept such a life. But his behaviour was a bit odd for me. My boss who initially introduced us, took me out for lunch and asked me how things were going? I thanked her for setting me up with him, as he was seemingly a really nice guy. She looked bewildered and told me that she hadn't woken up in the morning and thought to introduce us. In fact he had been on her case for days to introduce us, and that is why she invited me out for drinks and made the Pizza Express lunch happen. She told me that he had liked me, told her quite openly and he had wanted to be set up with me. I was surprised and aghast by what I was being told, but thought…At least this guy has guts.

Then, it was nearly October and my birthday was coming up. As you have probably gathered by now, I like to celebrate in style. My birthday is like my own national holiday, so this year I planned something out of the box and had booked a trip to skydive in Dubai. By chance I knew that he would be there around this time but I was in two minds to tell him. Sods law that I was on the phone to him when the travel agent called and he found out that I would be in Dubai for my birthday.

When he found out, he told me that he would be in China with a work trip, which was a shame, but I was okay with it. Over the next few weeks we chatted and he told me that he would actually be in Dubai when I would be, and he was looking forward to spend my birthday with me and would take me out for dinner, drinks whatever I fancied as it was my special day. I was bowled over with his romantic nature. As time went by and I was gearing up to fly, Am told me that he was stuck in India as his visa for a work trip to America had not come through. I thought it wouldn't take too long and we carried on talking about the trip and day-to-day stuff with each other as per normal. I was literally working away like a beaver until the point I flew. When I left for my holiday I had not heard a peep from him, a few days went by and nothing. Eventually he sent me a message after two days saying "As you can gather I am not there right now - visa issues. Call it a third world problem if you wish." I was fuming beyond belief, but carried on with my holiday. Eventually my birthday came along and after my midnight surge of calls from family and very close friends at twelve forty five he called to wish me "Happy birthday". He was laughing and joking like there was no big deal and I literally let rip. I told Am that I was appalled that he had not told me sooner that his visa had not arrived and was really unhappy by the fact he said all those things to me and did not follow through. What made it worse was that he said he "didn't remember any of it." Was the man suffering from temporary amnesia? Then after recalling the majority of the conversation, it was met with a "Oh yeah.. Now I remember... I'll call you tomorrow." To which I retorted "You know what... Don't bother." He was shocked and could not believe why I was annoyed. I am one of those people who trusts people and their word means a lot to me, I am perhaps a bit old school but a "gentleman's promise" means a lot to me. When someone does not follow through it makes me question them in my life and also their upbringing. But this one fell through when it mattered and that hurt me a lot. Nonetheless, I had a lovely birthday. My skydive was brilliant and I had my body pummelled and massaged to the point where I felt that I was walking on a cloud. But I did not hear a peep from the Freshie. He literally went into hiding and for the first few days I felt my anger was justified then I began to realise life is too short. But when I called him, he did not answer my calls and blanked my messages. Eventually after a week he rose from the ashes and acted like nothing was wrong. He was excited as he would be coming to London soon and was keen to meet. I let bygones be bygones and we went back to being normal with each other.

Before he came to London, Am had some work in France so we spoke and as he was busy with a conference it was nice to have him close by and felt like no love had been lost between us. I'll admit I did feel a bit guilty for my outburst but deep down felt it was justified being of a certain nature. I thought it would be best to bury the hatchet and go back to the way things were. When he arrived his flight was delayed and as soon as he got into the office, he was swept into one meeting after another. He managed to wink at me before he went into a meeting and when he jumped out to grab a coffee, I asked if I would be seeing him later. To which he said "Of course, as soon as I'm done we're going for a few drinks, then I am all yours." A few hours later, I got tied up with a meeting and when I came out I discovered from my colleagues he'd gone for drinks with some other colleagues; however not in the local vicinity. He'd headed off to South London. I was gobsmacked. Around ten o'clock he messaged saying "Let's go out." I was like, "I'm in my PJ's, no chance in hell am I going out!" He responded by "I want to see you. I'm coming to see you in a bit and let's fly away somewhere together." I just sat on my sofa laughing at the loon.

A few hours later he rocked up to my house and said. "Right, get your bags packed. We are going away." I had discovered before coming to me, he'd gone for drinks and then to another Christmas party hosted by another company. After that, he'd decided to call it a night. So I was not exactly impressed. Then he said Heathrow is an international airport and as he had a meeting at four the next day, we should just grab a flight and go somewhere and be back the following afternoon. I then informed him that Heathrow does go to sleep and would be closed at this ungodly hour so he needed to take a chill pill and relax. He proceeded to grab my iPad and looked ferociously for flights to no avail.

Then after surrendering his soul, we ended up chatting, catching up and truthfully it felt like nothing was wrong. We talked for ages and then he left.

The following day, he messaged me from his meeting to tell me he was thinking of me (a concept more men should do!) He then told me that he would be leaving for Russia on Monday and his trip to London would now be cut short.

I was genuinely gutted, as I had taken a couple of days off work in the hope we could spend some time together and I needed to get some work done at home. I then told him quite clearly that I was expecting some one-to-one time before he left and a SKYPE from the airport and air kisses from the sky did not count! He laughed and promised that we would meet before his flight.

The following day I did not hear a peep from him, the whole day went by and nothing, eventually the office closed and nothing. I then got a phone call at 9.45pm, and I was half tempted not to answer the phone as I knew his flight was at 10pm. He began asking, was I that angry to not call before he left? At that point I let rip. I said "Tell me something - you have friends all across the world, so ask anyone this question..." If there is one thing about Am it is that he always claimed to be "an analytical type of person". He was neither emotional nor ruled by his feelings.

I have dealt with many people like this in my life and thought it is about time I gave him a scenario he would never forget so I said to him "Am. I'm going to give you a scenario. You have a sister (which he did) so tell me she meets a guy at work, he peruses her, they get on great, they have ups and downs but generally more happy times than bad, he declares them exclusive.

Yet the only time he makes for her is at10pm, 2am or 4am in the morning. Is she:

A: *A whore*

B. *A hooker*

C. Time pass

D. Something else?

I then went on to say I did not mean to offend him by using his sister's example, but I too am someone's daughter and I'd like to hear from his mouth what he thinks of such a woman?

He then started shrieking "WHAT?! Are you serious?" To which I said quite simply "yes I am." Then he started saying if he made me this upset, maybe it was best that "we stay friends". It's a known fact I do not believe in this whole "let's stay friends" rubbish. Either you are with me or without me. There is no in-between. I counter-asked him "Is that what you want?" He did not even pause and replied with "Of course not!" In the middle of this very intense conversation, I could hear the air-hostess saying "Sir, please put your phone away. We are about to take off." So he had me on one side of the phone and her on the other. It was a laughable scenario, as her requests for him to turn his phone off got louder and louder. Then he told me "This conversation is not over. We need to speak face to face." When he arrived the next day I messaged to ask if he'd reached and he replied, with "yes I am safe and sound". A few days went by and nothing, at which point I called and realised he was blanking my calls, so I left it.

A few weeks went by. I was left feeling very confused and truly astounded how someone could be so hot and cold, bewildered how someone could turn their feelings off like a tap. By Christmas I was generally feeling quite tired the year had been so hectic on a professional and home front. To my shock and horror on Christmas day, he messaged me Merry Christmas. When I asked him how another miracle after the birth of Christ appeared on my phone today, he responded, "wish karna toh banta hai" which means one should wish another. After such a short response I informed him that on behalf of myself and Jesus, thank you for the wish and that he would be making an appearance in this book. New year came and went and not a peep.

I am a strong believer that actions speak louder than words and having dealt with a number of guys from the homeland I know they have the gift of the gab. This one actually hit me and hurt me hard because there was no real ending to the whole thing and I don't like people who can't be open and honest and be clear cut.

I firmly believe that regardless of where a man or woman is from you should not judge them solely on their words. You should judge them by their actions. I believe you should never beg someone for the things that you know that you deserve. In this case, it was, time. Admittedly the disappearing act was not something that I am accustomed to and genuinely hurt my feelings.

The right person will give you everything you deserve and things you never knew about. Sadly we live in a world where some people will just talk the talk as my Freshie did, but it's the ones that talk the talk and walk the walk that are the real keepers.

CONCLUSION

Well ladies and gentlemen that's the end of the story of me and my magnificent eight. I'll admit that I am not an expert in the whole love/arranged marriage process and do not hold a PhD in the subject. But there are a few things I have learnt and I will bestow some words of wisdom upon you:

1) Know what you want in a man - make a list of qualities if it helps figure out what YOU want.

2) ALWAYS dress well - you never know when you'll meet your soul mate. As looking trampy is not a good start.

3) Be open with your family, tell them what you want- They usually have your best interest at heart.

4) Don't say yes until you are 100% confident.

5) ALWAYS ASK FOR A PHOTO - If they say no, it means that they have something to hide.

The arranged marriage process is complex on a number of scales. However it does have its comical moments and its imperative to go into the process and remain open-minded. It's surprising how much something as innocent as meeting with someone can have such large impact on you as a person. It is indeed a great character building exercise and I must say it certainly builds up your tolerance for others and criticism. In life, you meet a lot of people and some people stick and some people will slide away from you, whatever happens do not change who you are, maintain your views and values. Eventually you will meet someone who is tired of the games and their loyalty, love and sincerity will match yours.

I once heard someone say that 'you have to kiss a lot of frogs before you find your prince' and I am certain I'll find my prince one day and sincerely wish you all the best in finding yours.